One in a thousand

D1712921

One
in a
thousand

The calling and work of a pastor

Erroll Hulse

PUBLISHING WITH A MISSION

EP BOOKS
Faverdale North
Darlington
DL3 0PH, England

www.epbooks.org
sales@epbooks.org

EP BOOKS are distributed in the USA by:
JPL Fulfillment
3741 Linden Avenue Southeast,
Grand Rapids, MI 49548.

E-mail:sales@jplfulfillment.com
Tel: 877.683.6935

First published 2014

British Library Cataloguing in Publication Data available
ISBN: 978-085234-913-7

Contents

Church history 85

Preface

Inspiration from biographies

D r Martyn Lloyd-Jones regularly urged the pastors at the fraternal he led in London to study the Scriptures in the mornings but to read biographies in the afternoon. He explained the reason for that. This practice, he urged, keeps the heart warm.

Through biographies and autobiographies it is possible to walk with and have fellowship with the great leaders that God has given his Church over the centuries. The benefits, of course, are broader than the warming of the heart. Church history is learned though biographies as well as through history books. How did the leaders of the past endure difficult circumstances? How did they organize their spiritual lives? How did they handle failure and disappointment? How did they meet the challenges of evangelism?

Early on when I was attending Westminster Chapel and sitting under his ministry, Dr Lloyd-Jones gave me a copy of *The Life of Robert Murray M'Cheyne*. From 1957 to 1967 I worked as the manager of the Banner of Truth publishing house, then situated in Chiltern Street off Marylebone Road, parallel to Baker Street in London. During those years two major biographies were published, namely *The Life of George Whitefield* in two volumes prepared and edited by Arnold Dallimore, and *The Life of Charles Haddon Spurgeon,* prepared and edited by S. M. Houghton and extracted from the large four-volume set of Spurgeon's autobiography. These biographies made a massive impact on me and even more so as I was very closely involved in the design, layout and illustrations used to present these books in an attractive format.

I have gained instruction and inspiration from many other Christian leaders. Compared to some libraries mine is modest. I keep biographies in a separate section and possess about 300. William Carey and Adoniram Judson are bright lights in the firmament of pioneer missionary work, as is John G. Paton. I was once asked to present the life and work of Thomas Barnardo, a Baptist minister who was a friend of C. H. Spurgeon. That brought me into the world of social conditions of the late nineteenth century.

Readers may wonder at the choice made in this book. Why not Spurgeon and why not Whitefield? One answer is that these leaders are simply too gifted to compare with us average pastors. Of course we can be inspired by them but I have chosen those who when together will provide a balance of requirements for pastors, such as study (Jonathan Edwards), prayer (Martin Holdt), application in preaching which is always difficult and so often lacking (William Perkins), evangelism (Richard Baxter), the primacy of preaching (Martyn Lloyd-Jones) and courage in reformation (Martin Luther).

If asked the question, 'Who has inspired you most over the years?' I answer, Martin Luther. I know and lament his faults but accord with Patrick Collinson, the well-known historian and author of *The Elizabethan Puritan Movement* (1967) who died in September

2011 aged eighty-two. For him 'the central European figure was Luther, rather than Calvin. Luther', he argued, 'changed the course of history not by building political or theological systems but by projecting on to the world around him his impassioned discovery that only absolute faith — not the good works and outward worship hallowed by the Church — can bring salvation.'

In this turbulent world we wonder how it can be possible that this earth will be filled with a knowledge of the Lord as the waters cover the sea (Hab. 2:14; Ps. 72:19). The sixteenth-century Reformation demonstrates how quickly massive changes can take place. The Reformation shows how God can take the most humble men and empower them to preach the life-changing Word with extraordinary results. The Reformation was preceded by a concert of prayer represented by the movement known as the *Devotio Moderna*. This was a spiritual movement stressing Bible study and prayer. The best-known leader was Gerard Groote (1340–1384) of the Netherlands. The movement was also known as Brethren of the Common Life which grew during the fourteenth and fifteenth centuries in Germany and the Netherlands. Working outside the official church, schools were established throughout Germany and the Netherlands.

Surely we must pray without ceasing for great spiritual awakenings. Indeed the promises form a basis upon which we can pray for global revival.

In writing this book I have had in mind the needs of the developing world, especially Africa where there is very little knowledge of church history. The example of former gifted pastors can be an inspiration to us today.

Introduction

The pastor — one in a thousand

In Job 33:22-24 we read of a man who is lost. He is drawing near to death. The funeral undertakers are not far away. The angels of death are ready to remove this lost soul to hell. Suddenly a messenger intervenes. It is a visitor who comes to the bedside of this sick man. This messenger tells him the way of salvation. He describes a ransom that has been made for sinners and proclaims the gift of eternal life for every repentant, believing soul. Hope is kindled in the dying man. He believes the good news of salvation. He embraces the Saviour. His physical condition begins to improve. His life is spared. His soul is saved. As Matthew Henry puts it, 'These joyful tidings delivered to him by God's messenger shall revive his spirit, and by degrees restore his former health and vigour.' But who is the kind visitor who has brought glad tidings? Who is this man of knowledge who cares for souls? He is described as 'One in a thousand'.

Where can we find such a man?

John Bunyan in *Pilgrim's Progress* describes the pastor as one in a thousand. 'Then he [Christian] went on till he came to the house of the *Interpreter*, where he knocked over and over; at last one came to the door, and asked who was there?

'*Christian*: Sir, he is a traveller, who was bid by an acquaintance of the good man of this house, to call here for my profit; I would therefore speak with the Master of the house. So he called for the Master of the house, who, after a little time, came to Christian and asked him what he would have.

'Sir, said *Christian*, I am a man that am come from the City of Destruction, and am going to the Mount Zion; and I was told by the Man that stands at the Gate, at the head of this way, that if I called here, you would show me excellent things, such as would help me on my journey.

'Then said the *Interpreter*, Come in, I will show thee that which will be profitable to thee. So he commanded his man to light the candle and bid *Christian* follow him: so he had him into a private room, and bid his man open a door, the which when he had done, *Christian* saw the picture of a very grave Person hang up against a wall; and this was the fashion of it. It had eyes lifted up to Heaven, the best of Books in his hand, the Law of truth was written upon his lips, the World was behind his back; it stood as if it pleaded with men, and a Crown of Gold did hang over its head.

'Then said *Christian*, What means this?

'*Interpreter*: The man whose picture this is, is one of a thousand; he can beget children, travail in birth with children, and nurse them himself when they are born (1 Cor. 4:15; Gal. 4:19).'

As we look around society in the twenty-first century, that man is a Christian pastor. He is one in a thousand. In many places he is one in ten thousand for there is an increasing shortage of godly pastors. A truly called, godly, caring pastor who loves souls and who unfailingly proclaims eternal life through faith in Jesus Christ is truly one in ten thousand. Take cities of a million souls. How many faithful, reliable, caring shepherds are there? The answer is: too few. You have to search for them.

The English Puritan, William Perkins (1558–1602), searched out reasons why there was a shortage of pastors in his time. He suggested that there is contempt in the world for those who unflinchingly declare the truths of the Bible and who apply the gospel to lost souls. Any person contemplating the ministry must reckon with difficulties. The pastor must be a brave man to leave the world of financial gain and worldly honour and take on a calling which is despised and often precarious.

The calling to be a pastor is awesome in its responsibility, as Perkins expresses it: 'To stand in God's presence, to enter into the holy of holies, to go between God and his people, to be God's mouth to his people, and the people's to God; to be the interpreter of the eternal law of the Old Testament and the everlasting gospel of the New; to stand in the place and even bear the office of Christ himself; to take the care and charge of souls — these considerations overwhelm the consciences of men who approach the sacred seat of the preacher.'

'It was this that made the apostle Paul cry out, "Who is sufficient for these things?" (2 Cor. 2:16). And if Paul said, "Who is sufficient?" it is no surprise that many others say, "I am not sufficient," and therefore remove their necks from this yoke and their hands from this plough, until either God himself, or his church, presses them into it.'[1]

Financial considerations often deter men from the ministry. God gave instructions about maintaining the Levites (Num. 18:26). Even though the office of a full-time pastor is deserving of what the apostle Paul calls 'double honour' which means double salary, too often it is the opposite and in practice turns out to be half or less than half of the average wage in the congregation. Why would Paul suggest double? The reason surely is that a pastor who is generous and active in hospitality and efficient in his work to reach out to all his people and to the community around him will have many additional expenses.

Perkins comments like this: 'The lack of such provision is the reason why so many young men with unusual ability and great prospects turn to other vocations, especially law. That is where most of the sharpest minds in our nation are employed. Why? Because in legal practice they have all the means for their advance, whereas the ministry, generally speaking, yields nothing but a clear road to poverty.'[2]

A good pastor is one in a thousand. Therefore, suggests Perkins: 'If their number is to be increased, training institutions must be well maintained. In order to uphold the kingdom of Satan, Antichrist is careful to erect colleges and endow them with financial backing to be seminaries for his synagogue.' (Perkins is referring to Rome, Rheims and Douai as centres of training priests for the Counter-Reformation.)[3] What would Perkins think of the phenomenon of liberal theologians today, who have destroyed many seminaries and turned them into institutions of spiritual destruction?

The godly, caring and diligent shepherd is 'one in a thousand'. Therefore it is vital that he should be encouraged by the prayers and support of the flock he oversees. Pastors are not dispensable. They are not there to be abused and to be dismissed for frivolous reasons. Such treatment can well lead to the displeasure of the Lord and cause him to send a famine of the hearing of faithful expository preaching. It is tragic when churches are deprived of pastors who feed the flock and care for souls with loving care, gentleness and wisdom.

Introduction

The need for pastors of quality is universal. It is well known that Bible-believing Christianity has multiplied to enormous proportions in many parts of China and there are other parts of Asia where churches have multiplied. The same is true of sub-Saharan Africa where some pastors are required to try and meet the needs of several churches. The short supply of pastors who can be described as 'one in a thousand' is alarming. It is tragic that many false prophets promote the prosperity gospel. It is their habit to rob naïve people. They ask for money in payment for prayer for healing. When healing does not take place they then demand more money, asserting that the payment was inadequate and that explains why no healing took place.

The scarcity of pastors in the UK is an increasing problem. The precarious nature of the ministry to which I have referred has resulted in many candidates for the ministry showing more concern for what we in the twenty-first century call 'perks'. Their first questions concerning a call to a church are about how much holiday time there will be, when and how long a sabbatical, and above all what the salary will be. While these are legitimate concerns for any pastor who must care for his family, the first questions should be spiritual. The man who is 'one in a thousand' will be concerned about the spiritual challenges in that church and how they can be met with spiritual weapons. What kind of unity prevails and what climate prevails for progress under the Word of God? What is the sphere of evangelism? What are the parameters of soul care? These are the primary issues. As expressed above, financial provision is important. 'If anyone does not provide for his relatives, and especially for his immediate family, he has denied the faith and is worse than an unbeliever' (1 Tim. 5:8).

Ignorant people imagine that a Christian pastor has an easy life. This book will illustrate the fact that the pastor, 'one in a thousand', will often wonder how he can possibly fulfil all his responsibilities.

These are briefly outlined in the chapter 'What is a pastor?' The pastor must be a fervent and diligent student of Scripture and of theology. He must be a man of prayer. He must, like Aaron the high priest, bear upon his heart and on his shoulders the names of all the people committed to his care. Moreover he will always seek the salvation of the unbelieving. He will always be missionary-minded and involved in the support of missionaries abroad. He is the caring visitor found at the bedside counselling that dying, despairing man described above. He indeed is 'one in a thousand'.

The chapters are designed to encourage high standards for pastors.

THE NEW TESTAMENT

The example of the Chief Shepherd in compassion and care;
The example of the apostle Paul.

CHURCH HISTORY

The example of Martin Luther as a reformer;
The example of William Perkins in stressing application in preaching;
The example of Richard Baxter in evangelism;
The example of Jonathan Edwards as a student of theology;
The example of Martyn Lloyd-Jones in preaching;
The example of Martin Holdt in maintaining a strong prayer life.

With regard to the example of the apostle Paul I have selected five matters which inspire pastors:

1. Paul's insistence on the centrality of the cross;
2. Paul's insistence on justification by faith alone;
3. Paul's amazing prayer life;
4. The practical example set by Paul as a team worker;
5. Paul's ability to endure suffering.

Introduction

Paul as a team worker calls for a comment here. The apostle possessed the capacity to inspire others and draw out their gifts and put them to work. This is a vital factor and it is encapsulated by Ephesians 4:12, 'to prepare God's people for works of service' (NIV), 'to equip the saints for the work of ministry' (ESV). Also the apostle Paul was mindful of training pastors for the future. He wrote to Timothy reminding him of the need to train men so well that they will in turn be capable of training the next generation (2 Tim. 2:2). Some of the most spiritually prosperous churches in the world today are led by men who have encouraged the gifts of others and trained men and guided them into useful service. John MacArthur Jr in California is one example and John Piper of Bethlehem Baptist Church in Minneapolis, Minnesota, USA, is another. Often pastors have to endure hardship and they certainly have to sympathize with those in the fires of tribulation and those enduring affliction. Where is our comfort? Our comfort is union with the Triune God. In Romans chapter eight Paul shows how the doctrines of grace are an immense source of comfort.

Each chapter begins with a biography. In this way readers can enter into the real-life situations of pastors. Christ's pastors are trans-denominational. The Head of the Church calls and equips pastors for his worldwide Church irrespective of denomination. The same pastoral principles apply everywhere. Jonathan Edwards and Dr Martyn Lloyd-Jones were Congregationalists, Richard Baxter and William Perkins were Puritans working within the Established Church of England. As for Luther he was unique and the father of worldwide denominations that bear his name. The contemporary pastor included is Martin Holdt, who was a Baptist.

Some may be surprised to find Martin Luther among the pastors. I demonstrate that he was indeed in every sense a pastor. He had no idea that he would suddenly be thrust into and be carried along by a reformation movement which would change the course of human history. Whether they like it or not, all pastors will discover sooner or later that they must work at reformation. There is a constant tendency for tradition to set in which can hinder progress. When traditional ways have solidified then any kind of change is frowned on and resisted.

I have chosen the Puritan William Perkins because of his emphasis on application in preaching. Most pastors confess to weakness in application. It takes a major effort to compose material for a sermon and that often consumes the time so there is little left to concentrate on the actual people who will form the congregation. William Perkins is the example to remind us of this need. It would be difficult to find anyone to equal Perkins in his helpfulness and in the skills required for effective application in preaching.

Richard Baxter is my choice of a pastor who laboured as an evangelist and at the same time pastored his people with zealous care. It is the responsibility of all pastors to engage in and promote evangelism. This is firstly out of compassion and constraint to reach the lost. As souls are converted, the churches grow and are built up. Additions by conversion bring encouragement to small struggling churches. I was called to the ministry in a small village church which had begun in 1772. That village church had declined and there was only one elderly lady member remaining. She was joined by a committed hard-working part-time elder who worked diligently to gather a group of twelve believers. I was then called to that village church on a part-time basis and eventually after five years to full-time pastoral work. We laboured in evangelism. The evangelistic effort was blessed with conversions and the church (Cuckfield, Sussex, England) increased to ninety members. When Richard Baxter began at Kidderminster the place was a spiritual desert. It was by the work of evangelism that the town was transformed over a period of fourteen years.

Lying at the foundation of all pastoral work is theology, the queen of the sciences. Pre-eminently the pastor must be a theologian. If he is to feed the flock he must study and be reliable and skilful in theology. Every Christian must be a theologian in the sense of knowing God. However, the word is used mostly to refer to those who specialize and there is no doubt about it, the pastor must love theology and especially as that relates to all his work with people. I have heard pastors claim modestly that they are not theologians. What they mean by that is that they are not theologians in the same league as seminarians who teach in theological seminaries and who write books on theology. My choice of Jonathan Edwards will, I hope, illustrate how a ministry is empowered when prayer is united with diligent study. Under pressure pastors can easily either neglect the primacy of prayer or the necessity of study. Jonathan Edwards was the greatest of all pastor-theologians in America. Before anything else Edwards was a theologian. His books are of immense value. Of all the theologians in the history of the Church, Edwards is esteemed as 'The theologian of revival'. I review some of the books that have given Edwards that reputation.

Preaching is the instrument that the Holy Spirit uses in adding to the Church and in building up churches with well-taught members. Theology needs to be transmitted and the best way of transmission is by preaching. I have chosen Dr Martyn Lloyd-Jones as one who inspired a whole new generation of pastor-preachers. If anyone doubts the primacy of preaching, the life story of ML-J should remove those doubts. Many regard him as the most outstanding preacher in the United Kingdom during the twentieth century. Such a choice may discourage those with lesser gifts. To allay that temptation I have sought to bring out a number of practical lessons designed to enhance the work of preaching. None of us enjoys the opportunities that were given to ML-J. Our task is to edify and build up those to whom we are called. During his lifetime Dr ML-J was an inspiration to many preachers struggling in difficult situations. He was a pastor to pastors. I often noted how sensitive and sympathetic he was to pastors who were having problems such as criticism and the threat of dismissal. He knew from experience what that was all about.

The biblical principles relating to the work of a pastor are the same for every generation and in every country. The ministry of Martin Holdt, a pastor in South Africa, has been an inspiration to many, not only in South Africa but abroad. In his pastoral calling he concentrated on the primacy of prayer and preaching. His emphases on the salient issues for pastors today conclude the chapter devoted to him.

1
What is a pastor?

There is no class of men and no profession under heaven more important than that of a pastor. Pastors are the spiritual eyes of the community. They keep open the highway to heaven and constantly call all to take that route. At the same time they warn about the broad road that leads to everlasting hell. For these reasons pastors suffer opposition and Satanic attack. Of this we can be sure, a faithful godly pastor is one in a thousand (Job 33:23).

And so the question before us is: What is a pastor?

The distinction between ruling elders and full-time elders is that pastors are called to leave everything secular and give themselves to full-time ministry. The preaching ministry is more demanding than ever before. Pastors are required to be skilled as apologetes as well as dogmaticians. Special gifts and skills combined with much labour are required to preach in an expository, systematic way which is practical week after week, in a way which captures the imagination and builds up and inspires a congregation. A minister who cannot maintain an authoritative, systematic, expository and attractive preaching ministry in an increasingly secularistic and pluralistic society represents a lost cause. Such work requires total dedication and full-time attention.

A pastor must have eldership qualifications. The two words *episkopos* and *presbuteros* are used interchangeably as we see in Acts 20:17 and 20:28 and also in Titus 1:5 and 1:7. Elders and overseers refer to the same office. The word *episkopos* is found in Acts 20:28; Philippians 1:1; 1 Timothy 3:1-2; Titus 1:7; and 1 Peter 2:25. The word *presbuteros* is used by James in James 5:14 and by Peter in 1 Peter 5:1 where he refers to himself as an elder. Before an elder is elected and set apart he must pass the tests set out in 1 Timothy 3:1-7 and Titus 1:5-9.[1] He must be called by God and have that call recognized by the members of his local church and the approval of the church officers of his local church. This vital subject will receive more attention presently.

In relationship to ruling elders pastors share equality (parity) but in leadership the pastor is first among equals. The New Testament addresses the subject of leadership in the churches. Two Greek words are used to describe the idea of leaders or leadership. The word *hegoumenos* is used in Acts 15:22 and in Hebrews 13:7,17,24, and is usually translated by the word 'leader'. It conveys the idea of someone taking the lead and acting as a guide. The word is used in a rather general sense, not referring to specific functions. The way the word is used in Hebrews 13 shows that the church is made up of leaders and those who follow them. The church members are exhorted to obey their leaders (Heb. 13:17).

The word *proïstamenos* is used in Romans 12:8 and 1 Thessalonians 5:12. It literally means standing in front of, in the sense of providing leadership or guiding. The word also conveys the thought of caring for someone with love. The same word also occurs in 1 Timothy

3:5,12 where it is applied to the need for an elder or deacon as a father to guide and care for his family. The focus of this word is on providing pastoral care and leadership. The word occurs in Romans 12:8 as one of the gifts which God gives graciously to the church which needs to be exercised with love.[2]

In larger churches where there are two, three or more pastors a team spirit is required in order that all the gifts are used to the full in harmony and unity.

Very few men are talented enough to sustain two occupations. The apostle Paul himself was so gifted that he could, if necessary, earn his living at tent-making and minister the Word effectively at the same time. Sometimes ministers are forced by circumstances to labour with their hands. In some countries pastors receive such meagre stipends that they are compelled to work on the land to provide food for their families. Jewish rabbis were required to learn a trade or some secular skill before their entrance into full-time religious work. Perhaps that accounts for Paul's skill as a tent-maker. This same apostle declared, however, that secular employment for pastors ought to be avoided, and he used the illustration of military service which requires total concentration (2 Tim. 2:4).

The difference between overseeing elders and full-time called pastors is the call to leave what may be for some a lucrative calling to serve as a minister of the gospel. A pastor is one who lays his life on the line. If things go wrong and he is dismissed from a church he and his family face a very serious crisis. A part-time elder faces no such quandary. Dr Martyn Lloyd-Jones was very well aware of this factor and was enormously sympathetic with full-time pastors and wonderfully pastoral and supportive of those in difficulty. It was the practice of Dr ML-J to restrict membership of the Westminster Fraternal to full-time pastors.

Let us take good note of the many examples in Scripture which show that men are divinely called to serve in a church. The Bible storyline is linked from beginning to end with accounts of divine calling to office. The more demanding the call and service required the more elaborate the divine calling. Hence note the phenomenon of Moses and the burning bush. Moses argued. He resisted the call. However, he was placed firmly in the saddle of leadership by the Lord himself. The manner in which the prophets Isaiah, Jeremiah and Ezekiel were called should be noted. Jesus was called from among men to fulfil the role of the sent Messiah (Isa. 61:1-3). He made this plain in the synagogue at Nazareth. With fury his claim to be the called Messiah was rejected by the congregation (Luke 4:14-30). By contrast we rejoice in the calling of Jesus as the sent Messiah. We note that the apostles were called one by one to leave their fishing nets and their homes to work as full-time disciples alongside our Lord.

The labour involved is described in 1 Timothy 5:17: 'especially those whose work is preaching and teaching'.[3] These labourers are to be given an adequate salary because, declares Paul, the labourer is worthy of his hire. The teaching elder is likened to the ox when it treads out the grain. The work is laborious. The verb *kopiaō* means to toil and Paul uses the word frequently to refer to his own mental and spiritual toil (1 Cor. 15:10; Gal. 4:11; Phil. 2:16; Col. 1:29; 1 Tim. 4:10).

Included in the gifts given to the Church following the ascension of our Lord are pastors and teachers (Eph. 4:11). As emphasized above, pastors are called to full-time work in preaching and shepherding. The pastor will be faced with the need of training. A pastor is different from the ruling elders of the local church because he is called to give himself wholly to the ministry. In that complete commitment he must dedicate himself to acquiring the skills necessary for the full-time ministry.

What about training for pastors?

When it becomes clear that an elder possesses the gifts and calling to be full time in the work of the church, what procedure should take place?

A variety of options are open.[4] He can join a local part-time training scheme and combine that with practical work in his own and neighbouring churches under the mentorship of his own church leaders. Or he can follow a guided reading scheme with his pastor, maybe calling on other local men with particular expertise in different subjects, at the same time as pursuing some practical ministry. Alternatively he can follow a distance learning course. If possible he can go to Bible college, either full time or part time. This can be costly and relocation will be an upheaval for his family.

Whatever line is followed, the fact is that preparation for gospel ministry requires *time*. In a secular context it takes ten years to qualify as a doctor, between six and nine years to become an actuary and about the same for a solicitor. Why so long? The reason is that preparing to enter any of these professions involves the acquisition of large amounts of information, understanding and skills. There are no short cuts — doctors have to know a great deal about how the body works if they are to treat their patients. Architects take six years to graduate. Add another five to that for an architect to go forward to be a qualified town planner. Gospel ministry is in this respect no different. It is more than the acquisition of knowledge. It is the skill to apply that knowledge and the skill to teach and preach week in and week out. Knowledge includes Church history which provides much inspiration from exploits of the past and also lessons learned to avoid the errors and heresies of previous epochs.

A pastor is required to rightly divide the word of truth (2 Tim. 2:15). He must have a profound knowledge of the contents of the whole

Bible. This means a clear understanding of the arguments and themes of each book and the principal issues which they address, as well as a sound grasp of how the Bible storyline unfolds. He must master the technical skills needed to get at the true meaning of the text and understand how to deal with the different kinds of literature in the Scriptures. He must know how to explain difficult passages. A knowledge of the Scriptures in their original languages is necessary. This all needs time — to study, to think, to pray, in order to acquire the necessary knowledge and skills in these areas.

The pastor then is one who constantly refines his skills. He is a doctrinal person. Why? There is the doctrine of the Trinity. There are the great truths of divine sovereignty and human responsibility. There is the question of the human and divine natures of our Lord Jesus Christ. There is antinomianism to be avoided on one hand and legalism on the other. The pastor must have a firm grasp of how Systematic Theology works. This will ensure that he teaches truth accurately and avoids heresy (Acts 20:29-31).

Training for gospel ministry should not take place in isolation from the fellowship and discipline of the local church. There are Bible colleges which guarantee that students are settled in a church fellowship nearby, where they can live, work and worship as part of a community of believers.

The example of John Calvin

Church history bears its own testimony with regard to pastors and training pastors for their work. John Calvin (1509–1564) is the most helpful. His greatest work was to train and organize the sending of pastors into France to plant churches. A similar testimony comes from Martin Luther who was a seminarian most of his working life. During the last ten years of his life Calvin

What is a pastor?

trained pastors. Eighty-eight were recorded as pastors trained in Geneva who planted churches in France. There were many more than that but for security reasons their names were not recorded. Eventually there were between two and three million members of the churches that were planted. That is an amazing record in the annals of Church history.

In Geneva Calvin established a four-tier system which reflects the way the Holy Spirit has worked throughout history.

1. Deacons; 2. Ruling elders; 3. Pastors; 4. Seminarians.

Full-time pastors emerge from the ruling elders and from full-time pastors emerges a small number of seminarians. Calvin called them 'doctors'. They are the ones who possess the gifts and calling to train pastors. Today America and South Korea provide the best examples of seminaries where pastors are trained for their work.

Necessity creates the need for the most gifted pastors to be seminarians. The best way to illustrate the necessity for training pastors is to describe how it has been achieved and the example of John Calvin is outstanding.

Geneva during Calvin's time has been described as 'the hub of a vast missionary enterprise'.[5] The city became a temporary haven for thousands of refugees fleeing from Catholic persecution in other European nations. Refugees came from Britain, the Netherlands, Germany, Italy, Poland, Bohemia and elsewhere. While there they studied God's Word in depth. When they later returned to their homelands, they were effectively Genevan pioneer missionaries, carrying the torch of the gospel across the continent.

Europe was largely an unevangelized, pioneer mission field in the sixteenth century. The unavailability of the Scriptures in the

John Calvin
Georgios Kollidas/www.shutterstock.com

common languages of the time, and the fact that church services were also held in Latin, meant that the vast majority of Europe's population had never had any sort of gospel preached to them in an understandable manner. Calvin spearheaded an evangelistic campaign which brought the gospel to the peoples of Europe for the first time for many centuries.

The majority of foreign refugees in Geneva came, like Calvin himself, from France. Although now settled in Geneva Calvin retained a missionary burden for his homeland. From the city of Geneva he sent out a body of missionaries determined on taking Roman Catholic France for the gospel.

A first missionary pastor was sent from Geneva to France in 1555. More and more were sent in following years, reaching a climax in 1561 and 1562. This missionary movement developed from a trickle in 1555 to a flood in 1561.

Research has revealed that 142 missionaries left Geneva for France in 1561. However, the register names only twelve of them. If that discrepancy is typical, many hundreds of missionaries must have been commissioned in the final period of Calvin's life. Of the eighty-eight missionaries whose names we know, sixty-two were French by birth. That means that twenty-six were cross-cultural missionaries in the fullest sense of the term. Nine of the eighty-eight were martyred.

When sufficient people were converted, a church would be constituted. In the four years from 1555 to 1559 nearly 100 churches were planted and constituted. By 1562 that number had risen to well over 2000. Underground religious networks of individual converts worked to bring in friends, relatives and neighbours. These were guided by professional missionary secret agents.

Calvin did not send uneducated missionaries back to the dangers of Catholic France. He believed that, to start with, a good missionary had to be a good theologian. He first inspired and educated them. The final assessment in front of the Company of Pastors included a test of a candidate's doctrinal orthodoxy and preaching ability. They examined his linguistic ability to verify that he was capable of interpreting Scripture from the original texts. The pastors also scrutinized his moral integrity, and questioned him on personal matters to satisfy themselves that he was of sufficient calibre for what was sure to be an arduous task. In addition to their studies at the academy missionary candidates were given practical experience. Some served as preachers in village churches around Geneva. Others worked as chaplains in the city or as tutors to well-to-do families.

In 1559 the training became more formal with the establishment of the Geneva Academy, under the leadership of Theodore Beza. This was intentionally set up as a missionary training college. Its express purpose was 'to train missionary pastors to plant churches throughout France and all Europe'. From this base, competent men would carry the gospel message to the nations. By 1564 the academy had several hundred students.

Only a careful distinction of offices in the church will preserve the proper functions of each. Where deacons take the place of ruling elders inevitably they end up doing the work of ruling elders. Where there are deacons and ruling elders and no pastor or pastors a decline in preaching standards takes place. This is a very serious and harmful lack as we see illustrated in the decline of Brethrenism. When everyone is minister, no one is.[6]

The advantages of the three-fold view, deacons, ruling elders and pastor are many. The equality of the ruling elders with the pastor or pastors protects the church from autocratic rule. The pastor does not rule alone. It is inappropriate for a pastor to implement discipline on his own. With ruling elders in parity there are checks and balances. The three-fold view encourages leadership. Unhindered by a multitude of concerns which are taken care of by the deacons and ruling elders the pastor can concentrate on prayer and the ministry of the Word (Acts 6:1-4). By this means the whole assembly is nourished as one writer stated it: 'Ministers are like the head from which proceed the stimulus, guidance and direction, which are essential for the vitality, the activity, the dignity and the harmony of the system.'[7]

Harmonious working relationships need to be cultivated among deacons, ruling elders and pastors. Confidentiality is important. Where there are differences of judgement humble submission to the majority vote must be maintained. It is important that there be in the establishment of church government a protocol which allows for dissent within the eldership — dissent without division. In our church meetings we often make decisions by majority vote, and we do not excommunicate dissenters. We all accept the principle that we do not need to leave the church just because the vote does not go our way. It is a great asset to submit to the judgement of consensus in matters that are relative. Before coming to a decision concerning a delicate and life-threatening operation, a surgeon may consult with a group of his colleagues about the procedure. In such cases the decision as to whether or not to proceed has sometimes been based on a straight majority vote. Thus responsibility for the outcome is shared by the group and does not lie on the mind and conscience of one lonely man.

Pastors and elders must at all times maintain humility in the recognition that they are related to the chief shepherd of the sheep and that they will have to give account of their pastoral responsibilities to him. Peter the apostle regarded himself as an elder and wrote as follows: 'To the elders among you, I appeal as a fellow elder, a witness of Christ's sufferings and one who also will share in the glory to be revealed: Be shepherds of God's flock that is under your care, serving as overseers — not because you must, but because you are willing, as God wants you to be; not greedy for money, but eager to serve; not lording it over those entrusted to you, but being examples to the flock. And when the Chief Shepherd appears, you will receive the crown of glory that will never fade away' (1 Peter 5:1-4).

In this book we will see that our Lord Jesus Christ, the apostle Paul, Martin Luther, William Perkins, Richard Baxter, Jonathan Edwards, Martyn Lloyd-Jones and Martin Holdt were all pastors. If we survey the small handful of pastors I have described we find that Martin Luther was a seminarian. He was a doctor of theology whose basic role throughout his working life was in the seminary. William Perkins was a seminarian who trained pastors for the ministry. Jonathan Edwards was recognized as the pastor best equipped to train others. He was called to go full time to teach theology in Princeton Seminary. Sadly he died prematurely just as he was about to take up that post. Towards the end of his life Martin Holdt devoted much of his considerable spiritual energy to training men for the ministry at the Afrikaans Seminary in Kempton Park.

By providing for and supporting seminaries and seminarians provision is made for training future generations of pastors. Thus the principle of 2 Timothy 2:2 is fulfilled: 'And the things you have heard me say in the presence of many witnesses entrust to reliable men who will also be qualified to teach others.'

In conclusion two important factors require attention. The first is a reminder of the responsibilities of pastors and elders. The second is the need to protect pastors and elders.

The responsibilities of pastors and elders

In addition to preaching and teaching the following factors are basic: 1. Participation in practical evangelism; 2. Visitation of the flock; 3. Attendance at the prayer meetings; 4. Gentleness and generosity; 5. Hospitality; 6. Absolute fidelity and loyalty to each other; 7. Affectionate attendance by the elders to the needs of the pastor and his family, and the encouragement of the deacons in their responsibilities.

After these basics the following responsibilities are to be observed:

1. The comprehensive spiritual oversight of the flock, compassionate caring, teaching and praying for all the members and adherents;
2. Regulating all gatherings for public worship including music so that it is not hijacked and controlled by a segment of the church;
3. Giving heed to all the flock by watching over them and praying for them; by organizing and encouraging the visitation of the sick, the restoration of the backsliders, the correction of the ignorant, and the guidance of those ready to stumble; the

encouragement of fellowship and the integration into union of all the members; the encouragement of full use of gifts within the membership (Eph. 4:11-12);

4. Overseeing the administration of baptism and reception into church membership; the preparation of candidates to present to the church and their instruction in all their responsibilities;

5. The rule of the church with respect to discipline by lovingly, yet firmly, dealing with those who refuse to fulfil their responsibilities or who are in a state of decline, sin or rebellion; the application of disciplinary measures when it is quite clear that all other means of persuasion have failed;

6. Maintaining the primacy of prayer in families and in the corporate life of the church;

7. Encouraging the work of evangelism in the community by organizing, leading in and participating in it; by supporting the planting of churches at home and abroad, encouraging the work of evangelism in all the world, and giving financial support in ways deemed to be most effective and timely;

8. Recognizing that the church is the pillar and ground of the truth (1 Tim. 3:15), the elders are responsible to see that the local church has an up-to-date and adequate constitution and confession of faith; they must think not only in terms of preserving the truth intact on paper for future generations, but also in a living way, by training up others who in turn will preach the gospel and train yet more (2 Tim. 2:2). In other words, elders must have eagle eyes to detect and encourage gifts, praying that future elders will be raised up for the church at home and especially gifted ones who may be sent into the world at large with the message of salvation;

9. Harmonious co-operation with the deacons of the church and encouragement of them in their responsibilities;

10. Maintaining unity with other evangelical churches;

11. Initiatives for evangelism and missionary enterprise.

With regard to the latter we should note that eschatology and church government are neglected subjects. In eschatology, which concerns the last things, we see that Jesus actually means it when he says he has all power in heaven and on earth and that we are to evangelize all nations (Matt. 28:18-20). We must realize that this is an achievable task in these last days (Joel 2:29; Acts 2:17). Planting churches in every nation (Ps. 86:9; Mal. 1:11) will only be achieved through pastors called to go to the ends of the earth to all unreached people groups.

There is need in the eldership for the recognition of gifts and functions which will continue the work of the apostles and their evangelists. Church planting did not cease with the apostles. It must still be promoted wherever possible in all the nations (Matt. 28:18-20). The church at Antioch sent out Paul and Barnabas to evangelize and plant churches.

Eldership is essentially a work of leadership which requires creativity, enterprise and aggressive evangelistic organization. This can be illustrated from warfare. Our Lord himself used such imagery when he spoke of storming the gates of hell. For illustration I refer to two famous generals, Rommel and Montgomery, who were engaged in a protracted battle across North Africa during the Second World War. It was a battle demanding extraordinary skill in the use of military strategies, and both these men were unusually endowed with genius. Montgomery observed the difference in character between types of soldiers. Some were better equipped for aggressive assaults, the storming of strongholds and the capture of enemy territory. Other troops, however, were better equipped to hold and defend with dogged tenacity positions which had already been gained and were not to retreat even under great pressure. His sagacious use of these character qualities in his men contributed largely to Montgomery's eventual victory over Rommel. In the spiritual realm, too, we need powerful and aggressive stormtroopers to do pioneer work in evangelism; and we also need those who are tenacious in holding territory that has been won and defending it against attack. What we do not need is men who are traditionalists, men who are unprepared to face the need for reformation. Traditionalists can be tenacious, but in the end they may be the cause of stagnation and discouragement.

To sum up, I note that there are those who excel in the work of keeping, caring and maintaining, and there are those who shine in planning and executing assaults on enemy positions. For its success the latter work requires an enthusiasm which is not likely to come from an eldership which is complacent and satisfied merely in maintaining the status quo, one lacking in vision and evangelistic zeal.

The protection of pastors and elders

Many a pastor has been destroyed by malicious gossip. This has sometimes come about because the elders were careless or wilfully negligent to obey the command given in 1 Timothy 5:19: 'Do not entertain an accusation against an elder unless it is brought by two or three witnesses.' In other words, there must first be definite proof before a case is even considered. Calvin's exposition of this text is so helpful that I reproduce it here in full.

> *Having given instructions about stipends for pastors, he now tells Timothy not to let them be exposed to slanderous attacks or burdened with unsubstantiated and unsupported accusations. It may seem absurd that he should state a law that applies to all men, as if it applied specially and exclusively to presbyters. For God requires in all cases that they should be established 'by the mouth of two or three witnesses' (Deut. 17:6; Matt. 18:16). Why then does the apostle evoke this law*

for the protection of presbyters alone, as if it were a privilege peculiar to them, to have their innocence protected against false accusations? I reply that it is necessary to guard against the malice of men in this way. For none are more exposed to slanders and insults than godly teachers. This comes not only from the difficulty of their duties, which are so great that sometimes they sink under them, or stagger or halt or take a false step, so that wicked men find many occasions of finding fault with them; but added to that, even when they do all their duties correctly and commit not even the smallest error, they never avoid a thousand criticisms. It is indeed a trick of Satan to estrange men from their ministers so as gradually to bring their teaching into contempt. In this way not only is wrong done to innocent people whose reputation is undeservedly injured, but the authority of God's holy teaching is diminished. And it is this that, as I have said, Satan is chiefly concerned to achieve, for not only does Plato's saying apply here that 'the multitude are malicious and envy those above them', but the more sincerely any pastor strives to further Christ's kingdom, the more he is loaded with spite, the more fierce do the attacks upon him become. And not only so, but as soon as any charge is made against ministers of the Word, it is believed as surely and firmly as if it had been already proved. This happens not only because a higher standard of integrity is required from them, but because Satan makes most people, in fact nearly everyone, over-credulous, so that without investigation, they eagerly condemn their pastors whose good name they ought to be defending. Thus Paul has good reason for preventing such a great injustice, and he says that presbyters are not to be given over to the malice of evil men till they have been convicted by legal testimony.

This principle is of so vital a nature that it should be included in church constitutions and should always be borne in mind during times of stress.

BIBLIOGRAPHY

Steven Martin, editor, *Biblical shepherding of God's sheep.* Day One, 234 pages, 2010. This book of fourteen chapters on different aspects of pastoral care and church life is highly recommended as essential reading. It is written by pastors who write out of personal experience in the ministry.

Conrad Mbewe, *Foundations for the Flock, Truths about the church for all the saints.* 338 pages, Granted Ministries Press, Hannibal, Missouri, 2011. This volume is extremely practical and eminently readable.

Phil A. Newton, *Elders in Congregational Life.* Kregel, 176 pages, 2005.

Derek Prime, *Pastors and Teachers,* The calling and work of Christ's Ministers, Highland Books, 269 pages, 1989.

Alexander Strauch, *An Urgent Call to Restore Biblical Church Leadership.* Lewis and Roth, USA, 1986.

Mark R. Brown, editor, *Order in the Offices,* fourteen essays, Classic Presbyterian Government Resources, 304 pages, 1993.

The New

Testament

2

The Chief Shepherd

The compassionate pastor
as described by Isaiah

The method I will employ in opening this subject is as follows:

1. The four Servant Songs of Isaiah — a brief overview.
2. A closer look at the first Servant Song.
3. The meaning of the phrase 'A bruised reed he will not break' explored.

The four Servant Songs of Isaiah — a brief overview

The Lord Jesus possesses in sublime perfection all those attributes which enable him to fulfil his position as Head of the Church. He is our great High Priest who ever lives to intercede for us. One of his titles is 'that great Shepherd of the sheep' (Heb. 13:20). Christ cares for all his people but he does so largely through his undershepherds

(1 Peter 5:1-4). The Chief Shepherd equips and inspires pastors. He motivates and energizes them in their labours. Daily they draw their strength from him.

As chief pastor Christ is the example or exemplar for those in ministerial office. What was he like as pastor in his earthly ministry?

His ministry is described in the four Gospels. The principles and character of that ministry are also described by the prophet Isaiah. Isaiah is foremost in the Old Testament for poetic brilliance. He is the 'Shakespeare' of the Bible. Divine inspiration shines brightly in his writing. He wrote four Servant Songs (poems) which describe the Messiah. The first, Isaiah 42:1-4, is introductory to the others. It begins with the word 'See!' or 'Behold!' Our attention is riveted to this one who is called the Servant of Jehovah.

Who is this mysterious Servant? Can we be sure of his identity? Cyrus, king of Persia (599–530 BC), is called the Lord's anointed and the Lord's Shepherd (Isa. 44:28; 45:1-7,13; 45:4). These four Servant Songs cannot refer to Cyrus because his role was political. He does not fit the picture presented. The nation Israel is also called God's Servant (Isa. 44:1). Israel failed to fulfil the particular role of servanthood intended, that is, to be a light to the surrounding Gentile nations. Israel does not fit here either.

The Servant who corresponds to these four Servant Songs is the Son of Man, the Messiah. He is Jehovah's Servant who said, 'The Son of Man did not come to be served, but to serve, and to give his life as a ransom for many' (Mark 10:45).

The Servant Songs appear in the following order:

1. Isaiah 42:1-4
2. Isaiah 49:1-6

The Chief Shepherd

3. Isaiah 50:4-9
4. Isaiah 52:13 - 53:12[1]

The first Song (42:1-4) is in three stanzas. In these stanzas we have a photographic album of our Saviour. We will return to this first song and view it in more detail. In a wonderful way the first song contains the main elements of what will be developed and opened up in the three Servant songs to follow.

The second Song (49:1-6) is autobiographical. This is the Servant speaking. Imagine in his youth Jesus coming to recognize himself in this scripture. This is the only scripture where the Servant Messiah expresses discouragement. The reason for his discouragement is articulated clearly and refers to the small impact made by him, 'I have laboured to no purpose' (49:4). This point of discouragement could be illustrated by the fact that when he was arrested his disciples forsook him and fled. It was only at Pentecost that his cause on earth began to move forward significantly.

The second Song begins as autobiography but becomes an interplay of speech, a dialogue, between the Servant and Yahweh. 'He said to me...' but I said, 'I have laboured in vain.' To that the answer is given, 'You will restore the tribes of Jacob and bring back those of Israel I have kept. I will also make you a light for the Gentiles, that you may bring my salvation to the ends of the earth'(49:4-6).

The third Servant Song (50:4-9) is autobiographical throughout. Here the Servant is introduced to the parameters of his suffering. How did the young Jesus come to terms with the shame and mocking and humiliation, the plucking out of his beard? Verse four is inspiring with regard to our devotional lives as we model ourselves on Jesus. 'He wakens me morning by morning, wakens my ear to listen like one being taught.' As he wakens he is sensitive to the prompting and guidance of the Holy Spirit. He listens. He receives instruction. In this way he knows exactly how to speak to the weary. He is ready for the demands of the day.

Is that how we begin each day? From the time we become conscious are we listening? Are we meditating on the Word of God? Are we sensitive to the pastoral needs that call for our attention? Are we thinking of the best way to deal with them?

The fourth Servant Song is the one we know best, and is more detailed than the others. The whole begins at Isaiah 52:13, with a call to behold Yahweh's servant. The first stanza provides an introductory outline of what is opened up in more detail in the next four stanzas of Isaiah 53.

I summarize the outstanding features as follows:

Stanza one (52:13-15). He is disfigured beyond recognition yet he will sprinkle many nations. This disfigurement is appalling. It is frightening. The assaults made upon him disfigure his appearance so brutally that it is worse than that of any man. Only Jesus as described in the Gospels approximates to this description. The first stanza introduces two themes, which will be developed in the four stanzas that follow. First there is his suffering followed by the outcome, which is that he will sprinkle many nations. Sprinkling has to do with cleansing from sin and defilement (Lev. 1:5; Num. 19:13; Ezek. 36:25). Today there are 237 nations in the world. In spite of efforts to exclude Christianity in some countries there are believers in at least 230 nations. In some instances the number who put their whole trust in Christ for salvation is very large. It is now accepted that there are more believers in China (about seventy million) than Communist party members. Yet while this idea of sprinkling is valid the Hebrew text is better translated 'startle'. 'And he will again startle many nations. Kings will stand speechless in his presence. For they will see what they had not previously been told about; they will understand what they had not heard about' (NLT).[2]

Stanza two (53:1-3). This stanza begins with the stirring question, 'Who has believed our message and to whom has the arm of the Lord been revealed?' How is it possible to believe in a failure? How can we believe in one who was tormented and crucified? That has always been hard for those who want a leader who is attractive. By nature we glory in winners not losers. We love the victorious not the defeated!

Hence the challenging question, 'To whom has the arm of the Lord been revealed?' It takes an act of omnipotent power, the strong arm of the Lord, for a person to come to faith in Jesus of Nazareth.

The Servant comes out of a humble background. He is from the stump of Jesse, a root out of dry ground. This exactly fits the Messiah who is the Son of David. As to his human nature he was descended from David (Rom. 1:4). The reasoning here is that from a natural point of view no one would believe on him because there is nothing in his appearance that we should desire him. This does not refer to his facial portrait but rather to the overall nature of his ministry. No painter — not Rembrandt, not Roualt (who is thought by some to be the twentieth-century equivalent of Rembrandt) — has depicted correctly the face of Jesus. Providentially his portrait is not known. No, the focus must be on his atoning work which is like a crimson thread that runs through stanzas three, four and five.

Stanza three (53:4-6). The emphasis in this stanza is vicarious atonement. The meaning of 'vicar' is a person acting, or appointed to act, in the place of another. Yahweh's Servant suffers and dies in the place of others. In this stanza there is repeated emphasis on substitution. There are sixteen personal pronouns which express this substitution. For example: *He* took up *our* infirmities. *He* was crushed for *our* iniquities. By *his* wounds *we* are healed. The LORD has laid on *him* the iniquity of *us* all. The punishment that brought *our* peace was upon *him* and by *his* wounds *we* are healed. He was pierced for *our* transgressions. The term 'pierced' is the same as is used in Psalm 22 where it says, 'They have pierced my hands and my feet' (Ps. 22:16) which is descriptive of crucifixion.

All this is the purpose of Yahweh for our sake. He was 'stricken by God, smitten by him, and afflicted'.

Stanza four (53:7-9). While the crimson thread of vicarious atonement continues in the words, 'for the transgression of my people he was stricken' (53:8), the main focus of these verses is on the behaviour of the Servant in his suffering. He is like a lamb led to the slaughter. As a sheep before her shearers is dumb so he did not open his mouth. Peter's testimony concerning the Servant fits this when he says, '"He committed no sin, and no deceit was found in his mouth." When they hurled their insults at him, he did not retaliate; when he suffered, he made no threats. Instead, he entrusted himself to him who judges justly' (1 Peter 2:22-23).

The sequence of life, suffering, death, burial (53:9), resurrection (53:11), ascension and exaltation (52:13-14) can be traced out in Yahweh's servant. His grave is not a common grave. Rather he is buried in the grave of a rich man. It was fitting that a perfectly innocent victim should be given an honourable burial. That grave was also practical in its geography as it was the means of making his resurrection as clear to the world as possible.

Stanza five (53:10-12). This concluding stanza begins with the repeated emphasis that this suffering was the purpose of God for our sake: 'Yet it was the LORD's will to crush him and cause him to suffer' and 'make his life a guilt offering' (53:10). As suggested above, the substitutionary element is sustained throughout this fourth Servant passage: 'He will bear their iniquities' (53:11). The last verse repeats that reality: 'For he bore the sin of many, and made intercession for the transgressors' (53:12).

However the main focus of the fifth and final stanza concerns the reward of the Servant. To what end is this horrendous suffering? The answer is that he will see his offspring. Jesus was unmarried. He was not a family man. His spiritual progeny is innumerable and is seen in all the nations, tribes, kindreds and languages of the world.

Commensurate with the severity of his suffering is the reward that is given him. Isaiah 52:13 and 53 is parallel with Psalm 22, which describes the anguish of betrayal and crucifixion followed by a description of reward. 'All the ends of the earth will remember and turn to the LORD, and all the families of the earth will bow down before him, for dominion belongs to the LORD and he rules over the nations' (22:27-28).

'He poured out his life unto death' (53:12). There could hardly be a more expressive way of describing the fact that the Servant voluntarily gave his all in the great purpose to redeem us from sin.

These four Servant Songs of Isaiah fit exactly the descriptions of Jesus in the four Gospels. These descriptions constrain a response from the reader. On his way home to Ethiopia from Jerusalem, a high-ranking Ethiopian eunuch was in his chariot reading this passage in Isaiah. He was joined by Philip who asked him if he understood the passage. 'How can I,' he replied, 'unless someone explains it to me?' Philip explained to him that all this has been fulfilled in Jesus and that by our union by faith with Jesus the cleansing and merit of Jesus' death are put to our account. That is salvation. The Ethiopian eunuch believed and asked if he could be baptized. The account is recorded in Acts 8:26-40.

The text declares: 'By his knowledge my righteous servant will justify many' (53:11). That means by a knowledge of what he has achieved for us we will be justified. To disbelieve is disastrous because that will leave us in a state of sin and guilt. Yahweh is extraordinarily sensitive about giving his Servant to such a death. We must embrace the Servant he has provided for us.

A closer look at the first Servant Song

Having given an overall view of the four Servant Songs, I return now to the first, and outline the pastoral ministry of the Chief Shepherd of the sheep. Isaiah 42:1-4 divides as follows:

Stanza one describes his person

a. My Servant whom I uphold
b. my chosen one in whom I delight
c. I will put my Spirit upon him
d. and he will bring forth justice to the nations

There are five points to note here.

1. *Whom I uphold*: What an assurance for Jesus to know that he would be upheld and his ministry would for certain bring justice to the nations.

2. *My chosen one*: Of all men ever born he is the one chosen by Yahweh and is his delight.

3. *In whom I delight:* The Father delights in the Son in the fulness of his being. He accords completely with his Son in all the attributes of deity and is pleased with the purpose of his mission to earth.

The Father loves the Son completely and perfectly. Hence at Jesus' baptism the Father's voice from heaven: 'This is my Son whom I love; with him I am well pleased' (Matt. 3:17). Again this love is expressed on the mount of transfiguration, 'This is my Son, whom I love; with him I am well pleased' (Matt. 17:5).

4. *I will put my Spirit upon him.* By the power of the Holy Spirit Jesus was enabled to fulfil his work. Conscious of this enablement in the synagogue of his home town of Nazareth, he opened the scroll of Isaiah at 61:1: 'The Spirit of the Sovereign LORD is on me, because the LORD has anointed me to preach good news to the poor. He has sent me to bind up the broken-hearted, to proclaim freedom for the captives and release from darkness for the prisoners, to proclaim the year of the LORD's favour' (Luke 4:18-19).

Jesus spoke the pure Word of God and in that context is described as having the Holy Spirit without limit (John 3:34). Throughout the Old Testament God spoke through his prophets and in different ways. Each messenger was inspired by the Holy Spirit. When Jesus came he trained his apostles and they were endued with the power of the Holy Spirit. The Holy Spirit equipped and enabled each apostle to fulfil his ministry or assignment. In the case of Jesus there is a unique fulness and perfection. He was endued with the Holy Spirit to perfection as the words of Isaiah 11:2 testify: 'A shoot will come up from the stump of Jesse; from his roots a Branch will bear fruit. The Spirit of the LORD will rest on him — the Spirit of wisdom and of understanding, the Spirit of counsel and of power, the Spirit of knowledge and of the fear of the LORD — and he will delight in the fear of the LORD.'

There is a marked Trinitarian character in the first Servant Song. The Father loves and upholds his Son and gives him the Holy Spirit without limit.

5. *And he will bring forth justice to the nations.* This promise to promote justice in the nations seems empty when we consider the atrocities committed during the twentieth century. The two world wars stand out as times of outrageous injustice. Particular reference can be made to the crimes committed by Adolf Hitler and Joseph Stalin. Through their barbaric despotic rule millions were persecuted and millions perished. Where is justice in that?

Running on into the twenty-first century thousands of Christians are martyred, mostly in Islamic nations ruled by mafia-type regimes. Where is justice in that? Serbian leaders guilty of genocide have been brought to account at the Hague but that is a very small proportion of the guilty. Where is justice?

The answer is twofold. First there is the prospect of the soon-coming universal assize or Judgement Day when Christ will judge the world in righteousness. Vengeance belongs to him. 'It is mine to avenge; I will repay' (Rom. 12:19; *cf.* Rev. 6:9-11; 20:11-15). Second there is the reality that justice has advanced and prevailed in many countries influenced by the Bible. In the USA, for instance, even animals are protected by law. Of course there are some miscarriages of justice but the instances of cases justly administered are innumerable. The administration of justice in the USA and the UK has advanced to the point where now sadly many seek to exploit the law. They litigate unfairly in the hope of financial gain. In Norway the law has been turned on its head in the case of the multiple murderer Anders Breivik. There the law is being used to protect him from the death sentence which he deserves.

With many countries in political turmoil it seems that justice will never prevail on the earth. That, however, is not what this text in Isaiah claims. Note the words, 'He will not falter or be discouraged till he establishes justice on earth.' There will be more comment about justice when we consider that promise.

The Chief Shepherd

Stanza two describes the Servant's unique ministry

a. He will not shout or cry out;
b. or raise his voice in the streets;
c. a bruised reed he will not break;
d. and a smouldering wick he will not snuff out.

'He will not shout or cry out, or raise his voice in the streets'. Isaiah 42:1-4 is quoted in full by Matthew (Matt. 12:18-21).

After he had performed stupendous miracles which evidenced the presence of the kingdom of God the people in large numbers were astonished. We read: 'Many followed him, and he healed all their sick, warning them not to tell who he was' (Matt. 12:15-16). It is reported that he did this on several occasions (Matt. 8:4; 9:30; 12:16; 16:20; 17:9). This deliberate concealment is sometimes referred to as 'the messianic secret'. Various explanations have been offered. He certainly did not act out of fear of his opponents. Time and time again he rebuked the hypocrisy of the Pharisees. Matthew 23 is an example of fearless, clear, scathing public rebuke of the teachers of the law and the Pharisees.

The reason for playing down his popularity was that Jesus discouraged a wrong and dangerous understanding of the nature of his Messiahship. Popular expectation could lead to the idea of a majestic, powerful, worldly figure who would come as the mighty deliverer. Even after the resurrection Jesus' disciples were thinking in terms of a political liberation of Israel (Acts 1:6).

When the Roman-backed Idumean King Herod died in 4 BC, the Jews sought social reforms from Archelaus, his son and heir. But the new king unwisely determined his power and responded to this affront by massacring thousands of worshipping pilgrims at the Passover. This shocking event produced a revolt in every part of the kingdom in the form of political movements aimed at the complete overthrow of Herodian and Roman control of Palestine.[3] Jesus' concern was that the crowds would interpret his ministry as the start of a liberation movement. He sought to restrain them. At the same time he continued to teach and minister in a manner appropriate to his Messiahship which was not political. As we see in the predictive description of Isaiah 42:1-4 his ministry was one of pastoral compassion and service characterized by grace, gentleness, patience, peace and justice.

'Not cry out' conveys the idea that he will not make a loud clamour. In other Semitic languages the term is used to describe the noise of a thunderbolt or a bellowing bull. Under this Servant there will be no screaming of orders or shouting of commands. His style was not that of military commanders and sergeant majors. His way was by soul-searching preaching that challenges consciences and thus impels inwardly and constrains the obedience of the heart.

This contrasts with some modern healers who advertise their healing campaigns and then fail to reach the expectations of those who come. When Jesus healed, his work was perfect. When he healed he discouraged any moves to make him famous on that account. A person may be physically healed but remain in sin and a state of eternal condemnation.

The Servant conducts a ministry of peace and is never advanced by the sword. The Crusades in the name of Christ in the twelfth and thirteenth centuries were an unmitigated disaster. They were promoted from the basis of superstition, the city of Jerusalem being regarded as an icon. The Crusades were propagated by an apostate Church, and the damage done has still not been repaired. Islam was offended by those Crusades. Islam is Jihadistic and warlike in nature and has advanced and overcome nations by the sword. That way has been and continues to be, 'Convert or die!' By contrast,

The Chief Shepherd

Christian discipleship is voluntary. No one is compelled by bombs, by bribery or by blackmail. Those who are not converted in their hearts are not converted at all.

Jesus' ministry is one of great compassion. If ever there was a bruised reed it was the widow of Nain. The only son of this widow woman had died. Jesus visited this town just as the funeral procession, a large crowd, was coming out. The heart-broken widow was weeping (Luke 7:11-17). Jesus restored the young man to life and gave him back to his mother.

Jesus' ministry is one of gentleness and sympathy, of meekness and humility. 'Come to me, all you who are weary and burdened, and I will give you rest. Take my yoke upon you and learn from me, for I am gentle and humble in heart, and you will find rest for your souls' (Matt. 11:28-29). All his undershepherds should display gentleness, sympathy and meekness. At the same time Jesus' ministry is one which is uncompromising about sin. He rescues sinners but his message is always: 'Go and sin no more.'

Stanza three describes the perseverance of the Servant

a. In faithfulness he will bring forth justice;
b. he will not falter or be discouraged;
c. until he establishes justice on earth;
d. in his law the islands will put their hope.

Every pastor labours in what forms a microscopic part of the world-wide harvest field. Every advance of Christ's Church to the ends of the earth is a cause of encouragement. Every setback is a matter of grief and disappointment. Sin and corruption have a vice-grip upon a fallen world. Even though there is the promise that our Chief Shepherd will be with us every day to the end of the world the prospect of success seems small. We are hopelessly outnumbered.

Like the despondent Elijah the weary pastor is sometimes tempted to think as did Elijah when he said, 'I only am left.'

The words 'he will not falter or be discouraged' presuppose that the obstacles are so formidable that it is possible to falter and be discouraged and perhaps give up in despair.

Jesus faced seemingly insuperable obstacles. He steadfastly persevered all the way to his death on the cross. He did this in a way that vindicated the justice of God as it is expressed in Romans 3:26: 'That he might be just and the justifier of the one who has faith in Jesus' (ESV). He endured to the end. By the cross Christ achieved our redemption, defeated Satan and established justice in the earth. His cross is the place where the sin question is settled.

The principle of justice was established by the death of Christ. The application of justice in the world belongs to him. That this is the principal meaning of the text is confirmed by the way in which the word justice is employed in the context, 'He will bring justice to the nations' (42:1). 'He will faithfully bring forth justice' (42:3, ESV). His kingdom will be upheld with justice (*mishpat*) and with righteousness. The Hebrew word *mishpat* is used about 200 times in the Old Testament and stands for justice. 'I will make justice the measuring line and righteousness the plumb line' (Isa. 28:17). 'Seek justice, encourage the oppressed. Defend the cause of the fatherless, plead the case of the widow' (Isa. 1:17).

He establishes all his people as righteous. Righteousness is imputed to every believer and then righteousness is imparted to every believer. Christians are the salt and light of the world. By them corruption is opposed. They contend for the rights of the poor, the deprived and the needy.

The long-term perseverance of the Servant joined to the fact that his gospel is to go to the ends of the earth and to the remotest islands signals the fact that his intentions are ambitious. He will not fail. His truth will fill the earth as the waters cover the sea (Hab. 2:14). This fact is encouraging to struggling pastors. However meagre they think their own field of labour to be they can rest assured in that in his overall purpose the Messiah will be successful.

> Kings shall bow down before him
> and gold and incense bring;
> all nations shall adore him,
> his praise all people sing:
> to him shall prayer unceasing
> and daily vows ascend;
> his kingdom still increasing,
> a kingdom without end.
>
> In all the world victorious,
> he on His throne shall rest;
> from age to age more glorious,
> all-blessing and all-blest:
> the tide of time shall never
> his covenant remove;
> his name shall stand for ever,
> his changeless name of love.

(James Montgomery)

The meaning of the phrase 'a bruised reed he will not break'

The crushed reed conjures up a scene where men and animals have been trampling a bed of reeds at the edge of a river or lake.

One tramp of the foot of the heavy hoof of a buffalo will break the bruised reed.

Yahweh's servant will not break a bruised reed or snuff out a fading or flickering wick of a candle. This reminder of the character of our Lord's unique ministry reminds us of the dignity of men and women, boys and girls. However fallen and hopeless, we do well always to remember that he will not break the bruised reed.

The flickering wick suggests a candle smothered in its own melted wax or one almost burned out. Yahweh's Servant will minister with supreme understanding of the helpless and vulnerable state of souls. With knowledge he will minister wisely and tenderly, gently, skilfully and compassionately.

These metaphors serve to describe the weak, the afflicted, the hand-icapped, the frail aged, the very poor, the homeless and destitute. Bruised conveys the idea of damage while the smouldering wick pictures weakness. There is a flicker of life but it is only a flicker.

I see several kinds of bruised reeds and smouldering wicks in which Yahweh's Servant, the master shepherd, is skilled and caring.

1. Jesus is the champion of little children

'Let the little children come to me, and do not hinder them, for the kingdom of God belongs to such as these' (Luke 18:16). In warning against sin, Jesus referred in particular to the vulnerability of little children. 'But if anyone causes one of these little ones who believe in me to sin, it would be better for him to have a large millstone hung around his neck and to be drowned in the depths of the sea' (Matt. 18:6). This is a reference to those young and tender in the faith who can easily be damaged. Christ is sensitive to those young in the faith. He will not allow the bruised reed to be broken. He will not permit the smouldering wick of faith to be snuffed out. Christ's undershepherds need to be careful to protect and encourage those who are young in the faith.

2. *Jesus is the sustainer of those under deep conviction and struggling on their way towards faith*

'When he comes, he will convict the world of guilt in regard to sin and righteousness and judgement; in regard to sin, because men do not believe in me; in regard to righteousness, because I am going to the Father, where you can see me no longer; and in regard to judgement, because the prince of this world now stands condemned' (John 16:8-11).

When the Holy Spirit is poured out he reveals the fierce wrath of God against sin. This can be terrifying. Can there be mercy for me? Is there a fountain opened to the house of David to cleanse me from my sin and impurity? Will I perish for ever? There is a Saviour who cares. The bruised reed he will not break! When souls are broken-hearted on account of sin, there is a Saviour who will not allow them to be broken. Bruised yes, but not broken; despondent yes, but not in despair (Zech. 12:10-14). Souls in the process of being drawn to Christ are like bruised reeds and smouldering wicks. It is easy to crush the beginnings of spiritual life.

A ministry of extraordinary skill is required when souls are beginning to emerge with new life. The picture of a smouldering wick is especially appropriate here. Yahweh's Servant will not allow that faith which has been kindled to be snuffed out. No! He will guard it and sustain it and build it up to shine brightly.

3. *'A bruised reed he will not break' applies to those who are weak or backslidden*

There are always in the body of the Church those for whom we fear. They are weak and sometimes show hardly any signs of spiritual

life. Will they persevere? In the past they have been zealous
for God and his truth and for his people, but now they seem
indifferent. A variety of reasons may account for this. Perhaps
they have been battered by affliction. Perhaps disappointment and
setback have made them cynical. Maybe discouragement has taken
its toll. Unanswered prayer may be a root problem. Often those
who are weak have compromised with sinful practices. They are
lukewarm. They follow on at a distance. We fear for them. Yet we
must remember that Yahweh's Servant will not break the bruised
reed. When praying for the weak we must plead the promise, 'He
who began a good work in you will carry it on to completion until
the day of Christ Jesus' (Phil. 1:6). Weak bruised reeds need to
be sustained and helped. The Scripture exhorts, 'Help the weak'
(1 Thess. 5:14). Weak souls must be the subjects of our prayers.

4. A bruised reed can apply to those who are orphans

True religion is to look after orphans (James 1:27). The world
is full of children who have lost their parents or who have been
abandoned by their parents who have not the means to sustain
them. This loss results in deep bruising and hurt. In Africa there is
the pandemic of AIDS which has resulted in millions of orphans.
The Christian ministry to these children is ever increasing in its
proportions. It is a ministry of love, care, provision and protection.
The spiritual challenge is to nurture these orphaned children in
the gospel.

5. A bruised reed applies to widows who are distressed

Widows multiply in times of war and those who suffer this loss
experience the very deep trauma of bereavement. Ministry to
widows is a vital ministry of spiritual comfort. Often wives
abandoned by husbands who are unfaithful and go off with other
women suffer deep hurt. The spiritual bruising is severe and Satan

is quick to take advantage. True religion is to look after widows in their distress (James 1:27). Pastoral care is essential and needs to come through mature women in the church who are encouraged by the pastor to fulfil that role. Christ will not allow the bruised reed to be broken. He will not permit the smouldering wick of faith to be snuffed out.

6. A bruised reed can apply to those crushed by disability

Our Lord ministered to lepers and to disabled people of all kinds. The constant burden of disability and intense suffering can bruise the soul and bring despair. Loving ministry is needed and one which points to the great consolations of the saving gospel.

7. A bruised reed he will not break can apply to those who are plunged into a sea of tribulation

Job said, 'If only my anguish could be weighed and all my misery be placed on the scales! It would surely outweigh the sand of the seas' (Job 6:1). Yet his greatest distress was his sense of desertion. He could not find the Lord anywhere (Job 23:8-12). At no point in his ordeal was Job broken in his faith. He was a bruised reed but not broken. He declared: 'I know that my Redeemer lives.' He declares his faith in the certainty of the coming resurrection (Job 19:23-27).

8. A bruised reed can apply to those who like Peter fail and feel themselves destroyed

The apostle Peter was broken-hearted because of his sin in denying Jesus. At that stage he could easily have been broken and defeated to the point of giving up. Gently and tenderly Yahweh's Servant restored Peter. A bruised reed he will not break.

Elijah had been in a similar place to Peter. Peter fell and then rose later to great heights of courage in public testimony to the truth. Elijah had risen to great heights in public testimony to the truth but then when disappointment came and Jezebel threatened a bloody revenge, Elijah cracked and ran for his life into the wilderness. There he bemoaned his loneliness and maintained that he alone of all the prophets was the only one left. He preferred to die than to live. He was a bruised reed. However he was gently restored and re-commissioned.

9. A bruised reed can apply to those who long for but are denied assurance of salvation

Believers who suffer from a grievous lack of assurance are like bruised reeds. They weep over their condition. They often suffer from depression which is related to their lack of assurance. For them we continue to hope and pray. Yahweh's Servant will not break the bruised reed.

10. A bruised reed can apply to those who are old and frail

Most depart this life in extreme weakness. I will illustrate this with one of my relatives who came to faith late in life. In an old person's home he became physically weaker and weaker. One by one interests fell away. At the end the only interest that remained was the weekly worship service. We cannot tell how weak in mind and body we will become if we are given long life. We cannot know what debilitating disease may strike us. The bruised reed is a symbol of such situations. Whatever our case we are comforted with this assurance: the bruised reed he will not break. I remember in South Africa, the land of my birth and upbringing, we were blessed with a pastor of outstanding spirituality. When he retired he lost his memory. He lived in a home for the frail. Yet even in the extremity of his illness he was able to pray fluently. The bruised reed Christ will not break and the smouldering wick he will not snuff out.

11. A bruised reed can apply to those who are clinically depressed

To be clinically depressed is to be under medical supervision. Depression can be very serious and often requires a time in hospital. This is an experience that can sorely try the faith of a believer. All kinds of doubts and temptations can enter a person who on account of the depression sees everything in a negative way. The situation can be so dark and gloomy that all hope is extinguished. Psalms 42 and 88 describe the dark night of the soul. For Satan these times provide an opportunity for an all-out attack to destroy faith, to break the bruised reed and to snuff out the smouldering wick. But Christ will not allow the bruised reed to be broken. He will not permit the smouldering wick of faith to be snuffed out.

There is comfort in this assurance for those who are suffering depression.

Conclusion

We have seen that the ministry portrayed by Isaiah of God's Servant is one of compassion. Jesus is the pastor *par excellence*. He truly cares and his heart is with the most feeble. As we have seen, his compassion is toward the bruised reed and his care is for those whose faith may be like a smoking flax. We have in Christ the Chief Shepherd of the sheep, the example for all undershepherds to follow.

3

The apostle Paul

Inspirer of pastors

I t is not overstating the matter to say that the apostle Paul is the most influential Christian in the history of the Church. He is the foremost theologian of the New Testament. Not counting the letter to the Hebrews, which does not bear his style of writing, Paul is responsible for twenty-eight per cent of the New Testament. The historian Luke is not far behind with twenty-three per cent.

Gresham Machen wrote: 'The Christian movement ... in AD 35 ... would have appeared to a superficial observer to be a Jewish sect. Thirty years later it was plainly a world religion, to almost as great an extent as any great historical movement can be ascribed to one man, it was the work of Paul.'[1]

Michael Grant in his book *Saint Paul* declares: 'Paul is one of the most perpetually significant men who have ever lived. Without the spiritual earthquake that he brought about, Christianity would probably never have survived at all.[2]

The life of Paul

Saul was born in Tarsus with the privilege of Roman citizenship. Tarsus was the capital city of the Roman imperial province of Cilicia. He learned how to make tents. That may have been the family occupation. He would have spoken Aramaic at home and Greek on the streets of Tarsus. We do not know when he moved to Jerusalem but we are certain of the fact that he studied under Gamaliel, a famous rabbi (Acts 22:3-4).

Above all Saul was Jewish. He was of the tribe of Benjamin, a Hebrew of the Hebrews. In regard to the law he was a Pharisee. As for zeal he persecuted the Church; for legalistic righteousness faultless (Phil. 3:5-6). On his way to Damascus to arrest and imprison believers a light flashed around him and he fell to the ground and heard a voice say to him, 'Saul, Saul, why do you persecute me?' 'Who are you, Lord?' Saul asked. 'I am Jesus, whom you are persecuting,' he replied. 'Now get up and go into the city, and you will be told what you must do' (Acts 9:4-6).

After the incarnation, life, death, resurrection and ascension of our Lord, this call and conversion of Saul whose name was changed to Paul is the most significant event in the history of the Church. The account in Acts 9 is reinforced by Paul's own descriptions of his conversion in Acts 22:3-16 and 26:9-18.

In Acts 22 Luke records Paul's testimony before an unruly crowd in Jerusalem. This testimony of the Damascus road experience is told in more detail before King Agrippa (Acts 26). Here we learn that there was more in Paul's calling than a short exchange of words. The Lord of glory commissioned Paul in detail. Here is the account:

On one of these journeys I was going to Damascus with the authority and commission of the chief priests. About noon, O

King, as I was on the road, I saw a light from heaven, brighter than the sun, blazing around me and my companions. We all fell to the ground, and I heard a voice saying to me in Aramaic, 'Saul, Saul, why do you persecute me? It is hard for you to kick against the goads.'

Then I asked, 'Who are you, Lord?'

'I am Jesus, whom you are persecuting,' the Lord replied. 'Now get up and stand on your feet. I have appeared to you to appoint you as a servant and as a witness of what you have seen of me and what I will show you. I will rescue you from your own people and from the Gentiles. I am sending you to them to open their eyes and turn them from darkness to light, and from the power of Satan to God, so that they may receive forgiveness of sins and a place among those who are sanctified by faith in me.'

'So then, King Agrippa, I was not disobedient to the vision from heaven. First to those in Damascus, then to those in Jerusalem and in all Judea, and to the Gentiles also. I preached that they should repent and turn to God and demonstrate their repentance by their deeds' (Acts 26:12-20).

'Paul's conversion was no gradual development, but a sudden and violent rupture with all his past thinking and activity; the light broke upon him, not like the dawn of day, but as a lightning flash, which revealed the glory of God shining in the face of Christ (2 Cor. 4:6) and at the same time illumined all other things and displayed his previous striving in its true character (2 Cor. 5:16; Phil. 2:7-10).'[3]

In Galatians 1:13-24 Paul describes a little of his life immediately after his conversion. He spent time in Arabia and returned to

Damascus. Then after three years he went to Jerusalem and stayed with Peter for fifteen days. Later he went to Syria and Cilicia. Paul steps onto centre stage from Acts 11:30 and is the principal personality in view up to the end of Acts. Acts 11:30 tells of Paul and Barnabas taking financial relief to believers suffering on account of the famine in Jerusalem. They returned to Antioch with Mark. Luke describes the call of Paul and Barnabas to the first missionary journey (Acts 13).

Three missionary journeys are narrated up to the time Paul was saved by Roman soldiers sent to rescue him from being torn apart by angry Jews in Jerusalem (Acts 21). From then on he was in chains. A salient feature of the closing time of his life is his unction and clarity in preaching the gospel to rulers like Felix (Acts 24), and Festus and King Agrippa (Acts 25 - 26).

Luke describes the shipwreck at Malta, where all 276 souls were saved from drowning, and they found refuge on the island. A viper fastened its fangs into Paul's arm and the islanders all expected him to die. To their amazement he was unscathed. Thereafter Paul exercised a healing and preaching ministry on the island. Acts concludes with Paul's ministry in Rome under house arrest. He was allowed to rent his own house and he continued his work. It is believed that he was released from that imprisonment in Rome but we do not have details as to what transpired in the three years before AD 65 which according to tradition is the year he was martyred.[4]

There are many subjects, doctrinal and practical, which can be taken up from the example of Paul. One of them is what he has to teach us with regard to missionary work. This is important because pastors have innumerable appeals for support for missionary work of which there are many kinds and most of them worthy. But priority must be given to church planting. Paul and Barnabas were called by the Holy Spirit through the church at Antioch to go out and plant churches and in due time set elders over each assembly.

I have chosen five matters of particular relevance for the consideration of pastors today.

1. Paul's insistence on the centrality of the cross;
2. Paul's insistence on justification by faith alone;
3. Paul's amazing prayer life;
4. The practical example set by Paul as a team worker;
5. Paul's ability to endure suffering.

Paul's insistence on the centrality of the cross

Paul wrote sternly to the Corinthians who were behaving badly. They had divided into groups following different leaders such as Apollos and Peter. The apostle reminded them that while he was with them he resolved to know nothing except Jesus Christ and him crucified (1 Cor. 2:2). Paul always preached the gospel within a trinitarian framework which he described as 'the whole will of God' (Acts 20:27). The cross of Christ was the centre of gravity in that whole will or whole counsel of God. Christ's work on the cross includes his suffering, sacrifice, shedding of his blood, priestly atonement, propitiation of God's wrath and death.

The gospel without the death of Christ is no gospel at all but is like a human body without a heart. The gospel without a crucified Christ is what leads to the health and wealth gospel which is the idea that Christ came to make us healthy and wealthy. That is a terrible deception. As his name Jesus (saviour) reminds us he came to save us from our sins. The communion table with the elements of the bread and the wine serve as a constant reminder of the centrality of Christ's death on the cross.

Christ's humiliation began in his birth. His humiliation is expressed vividly in the garden of Gethsemane. It is displayed in the injustice of his trials before the Sanhedrin, the Roman Governor Pontius Pilate and King Herod. His humiliation included mockery and flogging by Roman soldiers. Christ's humiliation reached its zenith in the worst death imaginable, even crucifixion. He was put to death by the worst of deaths, the death of the cross, a death of excruciating pain. 'The violence and the depth of pain were indescribable.' 'Now to have pains meeting at once upon one person, equivalent to all the pains of the damned; judge you what a plight Christ was in.'[5] The death that he died was violent, painful, cursed, slow and without comfort.

The worst aspect of it was that he was deserted, as we know when he cried out, 'My God, my God, why have you forsaken me?' His was a slow death pointing to the reality that he bore the damnation that our sins deserve.

In respect of men, Jesus' death was murder and cruelty and came by rejection, malice and hatred.

In respect of Jesus himself, his death was one of voluntary submission and obedience to his Father's will, 'As a sheep before her shearers is silent, so he did not open his mouth' (Isa. 53:7b).

In respect of the Father, Jesus' death was a death of providential ordering. As the apostle Peter stated on the day of Pentecost, Christ's death was by 'God's set purpose and foreknowledge' (Acts 2:23).

What Christ accomplished on the cross is explained by Paul in his letter to the Romans: 'God presented him as a sacrifice of atonement, through faith in his blood. He did this to demonstrate his justice, because in his forbearance he had left the sins committed beforehand unpunished — he did it to demonstrate his justice at the present time, so as to be just and the one who justifies those who have faith in Jesus' (Rom. 3:25-26). It is in the cross that love and justice meet. Love gave him and justice smote him. His death was vicarious, which means 'in our place'.

There is only one acceptable sacrifice. That is why Christianity is exclusive. 'Salvation is found in no one else, for there is no other name under heaven given to men by which we must be saved' (Acts 4:12).

In his insistence on the centrality of the cross Paul explains to the Corinthians why this is vital. Without it there can be no salvation. The point he makes is that the preaching of the cross is unattractive. It is gruesome because sin is gruesome in its nature and in its consequences. The Jews do not want a crucified saviour. They want to see miracles. The Greeks do not want a crucified saviour. Their delight is in new ideas (1 Cor. 1:18-25).

Nothing has changed. Today sinners are reluctant to face up to the fact of their guilt as sinners. The cross is the only place where the guilt of sin can be removed. The plea in postmodern society is that all religions are acceptable. But they are not. Christianity is exclusive because it is the only place where remission of sin can be obtained. Without the preaching of the cross there can be no salvation. Included among false religions is liberal Christianity which rejects the wrath of God and propitiation, and instead preaches the lie that God will receive people if they are 'good'.

Paul's insistence on justification by faith alone

Paul was insistent on the centrality of the cross and at the same time was uncompromising about the manner in which the work of Christ on the cross is applied to sinners.

In Romans 1:16-17 the apostle proceeds straight to the subject of imputed righteousness: 'I am not ashamed of the gospel, because it is the power of God for the salvation of everyone who believes: first for the Jew, then for the Gentile. For in the gospel a righteousness from God is revealed, a righteousness that is by faith from first to last, just as it is written: "The righteous will live by faith."'

We can see why Paul was not ashamed of the gospel, because it is good news. It is the power of God. He is actively at work revealing his righteousness. But what exactly is the righteousness that the Father imputes to every believer, from Noah (Heb. 11:7), to Abraham (Gal. 3:6-9), to every soul in union with Christ today?

The answer is that it is the active and passive obedience of Christ. Righteousness is everything that is right and perfect when measured against the moral law. It is this righteousness that is placed like a robe over every believer (Isa. 61:10; Rev. 7:9).

'Righteousness' is the word which sparked the Reformation. It is the word which lay at the beginning of a movement that changed the whole religious landscape of Europe. It was in an Augustinian monastery that Martin Luther exhausted himself in trying to find personal salvation. Then he was appointed to teach theology in the University of Wittenberg.

While expounding the Psalms he came upon the words, 'Deliver me in your righteousness' (Ps. 31:1). But what did that mean? The Hebrew for righteousness is *tsedqah*. Luther then turned to Romans 1:17, where the Greek word for righteousness is *dikaiosune*. Then light entered his soul as he saw that this righteousness is a free gift from God.

He testified that when he believed this truth he felt completely liberated; he felt that he had entered the gates of heaven. Also

Luther saw that our Lord was made the victim of *Anfechtungen* — in German that means a horrendous tribulation of soul.

So by his active and passive obedience, even under tribulation, Christ became *our* righteousness. 'God made him who had no sin to be sin for us, so that in him we might become the righteousness of God' (2 Cor. 5:21).

When we preach the gospel, the Father reveals a righteousness that saves. The verb in the Greek text is *apokaluptetai* — God's wrath is being revealed. The same verb is used for the revealing of his righteousness. When we preach the gospel, God is revealing a righteousness which saves.

The righteousness that comes from God can be called an 'alien' righteousness, because it comes from outside us. Say I received a garment made in China and I put it around me, it would be alien in that it comes from the outside, from another nation and culture. In its entirety it is not of my making.

Abraham is the Old Testament prototype of justification by faith: 'Abram believed the Lord, and he credited it to him as righteousness' (Gen. 15:6; Rom. 4:3). Salvation is never attained by works of righteousness that we perform; it is the free gift of God and received by faith alone.

The basis of God's justification of a sinner is the righteousness of Christ imputed to that sinner. The apostle Paul would have absolutely nothing to do with self-righteousness (Phil. 3:7-11). He grieved over the Jews, who were wilfully ignorant of God's gift of righteousness and went about to establish their own (Rom. 10:3).

If this is the righteousness which the Father imputes to us who believe, then it is surely appropriate that we should rejoice in the

Lord Jesus Christ as 'the LORD Our Righteousness' (Jer. 23:6). There can be no doubt as to the identity of this person. 'I will raise up to David a righteous Branch, a King who will reign wisely' (Jer. 23:5). It is he who is made to be our 'righteousness, holiness and redemption' (1 Cor. 1:30).

Following Romans we can define justification as an act of the Father's free grace to sinners in which he freely pardons all their sins and accounts them righteous in his sight, not on account of anything done by them or done in them but only on account of the perfect righteousness of Christ imputed to them.

In Galatia heretical teachers had invaded the churches and threatened this basic truth by teaching that it was essential for salvation to follow Jewish laws, especially circumcision. In his letter to the Galatians Paul declares that he is astonished that the Galatians had so quickly abandoned the gospel of justification by faith alone (Gal. 1:6). They had forsaken the foundational truth of the gospel.

He writes: 'I do not set aside the grace of God, for if righteousness could be gained through the law, Christ died for nothing!' (Gal. 2:21).[6]

The grace of God is gloriously displayed in the procurement and imputation of a perfect righteousness to repentant sinners.

That grace was frustrated by the heretics who were saying that the believers had to keep the laws of Judaism. In other words, unless the believers were circumcised and kept the Jewish laws they could not be saved. That frustrated or nullified God's grace because if we can work out our own righteousness we do not need the one that comes from God. Salvation is by grace and not by works. If we can be saved by works that makes Christ's death unnecessary.

The apostle Paul

Paul's amazing prayer life

In his letter to the Romans Paul begins by assuring the believers in Rome that he prayed for them constantly. This is how he expressed the matter: 'God, whom I serve with my whole heart in preaching the gospel of his Son, is my witness how constantly I remember you in my prayers at all times' (Rom. 1:9-10). Why does Paul take an oath in asserting the constancy of his prayers? In the words of Professor John Murray, 'It is for the purpose of assuring the Roman believers of his intense interest in them and concern for them and, more specifically, to certify by the most solemn kind of sanction that his failure hitherto to visit Rome was not due to any lack of desire or purpose to that effect but was due to providential interference.'[7]

John Murray makes a relevant comment that 'oath-taking is not wrong when conducted reverently and with holy purpose'. In reading the text we must note that Paul is specific in asserting that he truly did maintain a vigilant prayer life. He really was constant in his prayers for the Roman Christians at all times. Within those prayers were requests to God that he would be able to make the journey to Rome. That part of his prayer was eventually answered except that he was a prisoner under guard when he did finally reach Rome.

In the concluding chapter of Romans 24 names are mentioned. Did Paul pray for them all individually every day? We know from 2 Timothy 1:3 that night and day he remembered Timothy in his prayers.

Even though Paul had not been to Colossae he assures the believers of his constant prayers for them. With Paul it is not just a matter of much praying. There is quality in his intercession. Note how he prayed for the Colossians: 'For this reason, since the day we heard about you, we have not stopped praying for you and asking God to fill you with the knowledge of his will through all spiritual wisdom and understanding. And we pray this in order that you may live a life worthy of the Lord and may please him in every way: bearing fruit in every good work, growing in the knowledge of God, being strengthened with all power according to his glorious might so that you may have great endurance and patience, and joyfully giving thanks to the Father, who has qualified you to share in the inheritance of the saints in the kingdom of light. For he has rescued us from the dominion of darkness and brought us into the kingdom of the Son he loves, in whom we have redemption, the forgiveness of sins' (Col. 1:9-14).

In speaking in the plural he is including Epaphras his fellow-worker whom he describes as 'a wrestler in prayer' for the Colossians (Col. 4:12). The description of a wrestler certainly portrays Paul as an intercessor. We should think of Paul and Epaphras and perhaps others with them wrestling in prayer.

It is evident that Paul's prayers were not simply constant repetitions of places and people. He prayed in detail about the spiritual growth of the Christians. He prayed that the Philippians would abound in love more and more (Phil. 1:9-11). In his prayers for the Ephesians Paul soars to the heights in detailed requests for their spiritual growth (Eph. 1:15-23; 3:14-21).

Persistent constant prayer is not for super Christians only. We are all exhorted by Paul to 'always keep on praying for all the saints' (Eph. 6:18). All the saints? Does that not ask for too much? We could not possibly do that today because the worldwide Church consists of many millions among about 270 nations of the world. We solve this problem by praying for the believers we know and the churches we know and we can do that with some detail. And then we can pray in general for nations where persecution is rife. And we also pray in general for countries where the gospel is advancing such as Indonesia and China. The volume *OPERATION WORLD* provides masses of information to inform intelligent prayer.[8]

Paul testified that he faced daily the pressure of his concern for all the churches (2 Cor. 11:28). The Philippians were assured of Paul's prayers. This is how this assurance is expressed: 'I thank my God every time I remember you. In all my prayers for all of you, I always pray with joy because of your partnership in the gospel from the first day until now, being confident of this, that he who began a good work in you will carry it on to completion until the day of Christ Jesus' (Phil. 1:3-6).

From Paul's example pastors should be inspired to pray daily for all members of the church and congregation. They should be constant, faithful and fervent in their prayers for missionaries and for other pastors and churches. Some order will be needed when the prayer needs are numerous. A weekly prayer list will be helpful to make prayer a practical discipline. The danger is to be mechanical. We are to 'pray in the Spirit' and need to worship and be thankful before we make petitions. I keep a prayer diary in which I make it a rule never to record a request without first expressing gratitude for answered prayer.

The practical example set by Paul as a team worker

Paul spearheaded the missionary advance of the Church and simultaneously through his letters became the chief exponent of Christ. About a quarter of the New Testament came from his pen. Paul is not only the foremost theologian of Christianity, he is also her foremost missionary. The New Testament letters are all written within a missionary context. The pastoral epistles of 1 and 2 Timothy and Titus contain instructions about church government and how to recognize and appoint elders and deacons. I Timothy 5:17 refers to a particular kind of elder whose work is preaching and teaching. This reminds us of the fact that there is always a diversity of gifts among the elders. Furthermore there are full-time elders and part-time elders.

In small churches there is a danger of just one pastor taking sole command and becoming authoritarian. I have heard a pastor claiming that the church he led was 'his' church! Surely the churches belong to our Lord (Rev. 2 - 3). The danger is that a single pastor can use his power to manipulate the church to suit his needs. The New Testament tells of a plurality of elders. Leadership by its very nature requires that one in a church takes the lead but a true leader will make sure that the gifts and abilities of the elders are fully employed to the good of the church and the glory of God. When elders meet together there is equality. This parity or equality can too easily threaten a pastor's leadership which is why some resist the doctrine of a plurality of elders. But it is wrong to stifle the gifts that the Lord gives to his people for their leadership and organization.

A related problem is that of those who imagine that they are gifted but are not. They press for recognition. Romans 12:3 is the key passage here. Paul urges: 'Do not think of yourself more highly than you ought, but rather think of yourself with sober judgement, in accordance with the measure of faith God has given you.'

Paul was supreme in his giftedness. Yet he did not act like a pope. This claim seems to be contradicted by the way he differed from Barnabas over the role of Mark. Our Lord sent out the seventy disciples two by two. The Holy Spirit endorses this principle in calling both Paul and Barnabas to the first missionary journey. They chose to take Mark, the cousin of Barnabas, to travel with them. When the going was rough in Pamphylia Mark deserted them. Later when the second missionary journey was under way Barnabas wished to take Mark with them but Paul disagreed. This disagreement was so sharp that they parted and two separate missionary journeys were undertaken, Paul and Silas on one and Barnabas and Mark on the other (Acts 15:16-41).

This saga early in Paul's ministry should not prejudice us against him. Rather we should look at how his work developed. Paul's overall record demonstrates that he enjoyed the blessing of team work. He laboured enterprisingly in harmony with co-workers. The difference between Paul and Barnabas highlights just how important it is to work in unity and also to provide for means to defuse disagreement. Later we find that Paul was reconciled to Mark. To Timothy he wrote, 'Get Mark and bring him with you, because he is helpful to me in my ministry' (2 Tim. 4:11).

As the churches multiplied so a team of workers trained by Paul emerged. That these men travelled with him is seen by Acts 20:4. Mentioned are 'Sopater son of Pyrrhus from Berea, Aristarchus and Secundus from Thessalonica, Gaius from Derbe, Timothy also, and Tychicus and Trophimus from the province of Asia'. We know by cross-references that these were gospel workers. For instance Tychicus is described as 'a faithful minister and fellow-servant' (Col. 4:7).

Paul did not act as though he had to control everything in papal fashion. In Acts 17:14 we read that the brothers immediately sent Paul to the coast, but Silas and Timothy stayed at Berea. Here is an example of the brothers, that is, Paul's fellow-workers, telling him what he had to do. Paul did confer not only with fellow-workers but with the church family as a whole. An example of this is found in Acts 21:10-14. They all did their best to persuade Paul not to go to Jerusalem. In this case he was determined to go even though it would endanger his life, but this was certainly not a case of Paul's holding himself above the counsel of others.

Some fellow-workers like Epaphras suffered imprisonment with Paul. Epaphras planted the church at Colossae as we see from the text: 'Since the day you heard it and understood God's grace in all its truth. You learned it from Epaphras, our dear fellow-servant, who is a faithful minister of Christ on our behalf, and who also told us of your love in the Spirit' (Col. 1:7-8). Epaphras is described by Paul as 'always wrestling in prayer for you, that you may stand firm in all the will of God, mature and fully assured' (Col. 4:12).

That Paul worked with others as partners is seen in the way he addresses the churches. Thessalonica is an example where he begins as follows: 'Paul, Silas and Timothy, to the church of the Thessalonians' (2 Thess. 1:1).

When that epic voyage to Italy began which ended in shipwreck on the island of Malta, Luke is careful to report that Aristarchus of Macedonia was with them.

As Paul took the lead it seems clear that others learned from his example. He inspired his fellow-workers. By the way in which he writes to Timothy we can see how close together they were in their ministry. Paul writes: 'You, however, know all about my teaching, my way of life, my purpose, faith, patience, love, endurance, persecutions, sufferings — what kinds of things happened to me in Antioch, Iconium and Lystra, the persecutions I endured' (2 Tim. 3:10-11).

We too should be willing like Paul to work with others even though that may be challenging, especially when we are called to work with strong-minded gifted co-workers. Also we should become transcultural communicators of the gospel.

Paul's ability to endure suffering

Paul gives us an example of patient endurance of sufferings for the sake of the gospel. He endured pain and persecution, beatings and imprisonments, but not once do we find him drawing back from his calling.

Pastors and their wives will suffer all kinds of disappointments, opposition and in some countries aggressive persecution. In some countries like Mexico and Colombia pastors are exposed to the threat of violence from Mafia gangs. The lack of success in the ministry is often the cause of distress. Suffering is a part of the process by which the children of God are made holy. The Lord whom they serve was a Man of sorrows and acquainted with grief.

The undershepherds of God's sheep know discipline and are chastened, which is part of their becoming partakers of God's holiness. Their experience gives them empathy with those who suffer. The Captain of their salvation was made 'perfect through suffering' (Heb. 2:10; 12:10). As we survey Church history we are often impressed with the fact that those whom the Lord has used experienced unusual afflictions or endured great hardships.

How does the apostle to the Gentiles inspire us? The answer is by his example. Remember his example at Lystra where he was stoned. He was dragged out of the city. They thought he was dead. It seemed that the end had come. But he stood up on his feet. He survived. Following this trauma he did not take a holiday or a sabbatical to recover. He returned immediately to his work of preaching (Acts 14:19-21). He simply continued with his mission. At one point in defence of his calling he described his experiences as follows:

> *What anyone else dares to boast about — I am speaking as a fool — I also dare to boast about. Are they Hebrews? So am I.*

Are they Israelites? So am I. Are they Abraham's descendants? So am I. Are they servants of Christ? (I am out of my mind to talk like this.) I am more. I have worked much harder, been in prison more frequently, been flogged more severely, and been exposed to death again and again. Five times I received from the Jews the forty lashes minus one. Three times I was beaten with rods, once I was stoned, three times I was shipwrecked, I spent a night and a day in the open sea, I have been constantly on the move. I have been in danger from rivers, in danger from bandits, in danger from my own countrymen, in danger from Gentiles; in danger in the city, in danger in the country, in danger at sea; and in danger from false believers. I have laboured and toiled and have often gone without sleep; I have known hunger and thirst and have often gone without food; I have been cold and naked. Besides everything else, I face daily the pressure of my concern for all the churches

(2 Cor. 11:21-28).

There must surely have been a limit for Paul? How much more could he endure? The genius of his devotional life was his experimental unity with Christ. Our Lord, who called him to suffer so much, sustained him as we see when he was Corinth. 'One night the Lord spoke to Paul in a vision: "Do not be afraid; keep on speaking, do not be silent. For I am with you, and no one is going to attack and harm you, because I have many people in this city"' (Acts 18:9-10).

A further factor in Paul's life was the personal physical disadvantage that he carried. On the basis of Galatians 4:15 and 6:11, a case can be made that the thorn in Paul's life was an eye disease. We cannot prove it but that is the closest we can get. Whatever the thorn was, he suggests a reason for it:

To keep me from becoming conceited because of these surpassingly great revelations, there was given me a thorn in my flesh, a messenger of Satan, to torment me. Three times I pleaded with the Lord to take it away from me. But he said to me, 'My grace is sufficient for you, for my power is made perfect in weakness.' Therefore I will boast all the more gladly about my weaknesses, so that Christ's power may rest on me. That is why, for Christ's sake, I delight in weaknesses, in insults, in hardships, in persecutions, in difficulties. For when I am weak, then I am strong

(2 Cor. 12:7-10).

Pride is a terrible danger in a successful minister. If we should experience revival for which we have prayed we will need to take great care to give God all the glory and not ascribe any glory to ourselves.

How could Paul persevere through so many severe trials? I will conclude by going to the very heart of the Romans letter. In chapter eight Paul provides three reasons for comfort. First, our present sufferings are not worth comparing to the glory that will be revealed. Second, the Holy Spirit enables us to pray when we are distraught. Third, he assures us that all things work for our good.

'And we know that in all things God works for the good of those who love him, who have been called according to his purpose' (Rom. 8:28). This purpose of the Father is described by way of five actions joined together like links in a chain, sometimes referred to as the golden chain. Believers have been introduced as those who love God and for whom all things most certainly work together for good. So what are the five actions of God the Father?

1. *He loved us;*
2. *He predestined us;*
3. *He called us;*
4. *He justified us;*
5. *He glorified us.*

These actions are sovereign in the sense that God is active and we are passive.[9] They are gracious actions because as sinners and rebels we deserve nothing except condemnation.

J. C. Ryle wrote: 'Of all the doctrines of the Bible, none is so offensive to human nature as the doctrine of God's sovereignty.'[10] This truth offends because it means that as a sinner I am so bad that I cannot save myself and indeed am so bad that I cannot even contribute any merit to my salvation. The most common idea of a contribution to my salvation is my free will. I chose God and so he saved me. However, that is not what Paul teaches.

The Father's actions are gracious. Hence the expression 'sovereign grace'. Paul's calling on the road to Damascus illustrates the sovereign grace of God. Here was an outrageous persecutor of the churches on a mission of further persecution, but he was turned around and radically changed. The word grace (unmerited favour) is the right word to describe Paul's calling. I will expound just the first of the five actions outlined above because it is that first action that is disputed.

He loved us

The text declares: 'For whom he foreknew'. Many take this to mean that this simply means that God foreknew the fact that some would believe and so he predestined them to glory. That cannot be correct for two reasons.

Firstly, the Hebraic meaning of foreknowledge is implicit in New Testament usage. The idea is of an intimate relationship. It is persons that are in view not human decisions or events. This is expressed powerfully in 1 Peter 1:20 where Christ in his person is described as foreknown: 'For he was foreknown before the foundation of the world, but has appeared in these last times for the sake of you' (NASB). The NIV translates, 'He was chosen before the creation of the world.' Peter speaks of God's foreknowledge of Christ in terms of choosing and appointing him to be our Redeemer. In the introduction Peter describes the elect as those who have been chosen according to the foreknowledge of God the Father. In other words, they are beloved of God the Father. To know means to know intimately. 'I know my sheep and am known of mine.' Thus Paul strongly rejects the idea that the Lord has cast away a people that *he foreknew* (Rom. 11:2). That does not mean a people whom he merely knew about. It means a people upon whom he set his love.

The above meaning of intimate knowledge is conveyed by Amos 3:2 (ESV): 'You only have I known of all the families of the earth.' Also Hosea uses the term 'to know' to refer to a marriage relationship, 'I knew you in the wilderness, in the land of great drought.' In that terrible experience in the wilderness Jehovah was joined to his people. The verb *Yada* often carries considerable depth of meaning in the Old Testament, conveying the idea of a deep relationship of love. There is a lament when this kind of knowledge of love is absent (Hos. 4:1 and 6:6). This love is confirmed by Jeremiah, 'The LORD says, "Before I formed you in the womb I knew you, before you were born I set you apart; I appointed you as a prophet to the nations"' (Jer. 1:5).

Secondly, there is the consideration of parallel passages which explain precisely the actions of God the Father. 'For he chose us in him before the creation of the world to be holy and blameless in his sight. In love he predestined us to be adopted as his sons through Jesus Christ' (Eph. 1:4-5). The grace given to us has its spring in the love of God the Father (2 Thess. 2:16). The Father has given a people to Christ (John 6:37). Christ's love for his people is concurrent with that of his Father. It is this love that sustained

Christ in his determination to go through with the crucifixion (Rom. 5:6-8; 8:37; Heb. 12:2; Gal. 2:20).

A pastor finds comfort in the knowledge that nothing can separate him from God's love and the same applies to his flock. He can comfort them with this assurance.

Pastors are strengthened by the truth of predestination. God's purpose will not fail. Whatever the struggles, fears and sufferings experienced by the pastor in his work he can be comforted in the knowledge that in Christ he is more than conqueror.

Church
history

Martin Luther

4

Martin Luther and reformation

O f all leaders in the history of Christ's Church I have personally derived more inspiration from Martin Luther than from any other. A leader of his calibre is extremely rare and the kind of scenario into which he was thrust is unique. He never sat down and thought of a strategy as pastors of local churches do. He merely wished to debate crucial issues. In nailing the ninety-five theses to the door of the Castle Church in Wittenberg he was simply hoping to organize a constructive debate. What followed was like a tornado. From then on he was overtaken by events. From 1517 onwards he responded to one crisis after another as best he could through his writings.

Luther succeeded in attaining outstanding clarity about the way of salvation as the free gift of God received by faith alone, that faith being real trust in Christ and not mere assent of the mind. Little wonder then that Satan has done his level best to vilify Luther as a profligate drunkard, an idea that held sway in the Roman Catholic Church until reliable scholarship blew such nonsense away, as I will show presently. In recent times Luther has been criticized as a persecutor of Jews. He was master of hyperbole, but it is regrettable that that let him down in some instances. Luther's impatience with the Jews and his intemperate language concerning them is deplorable and is totally unacceptable, but we must not allow that to obscure the magnificence of his stand for the gospel. A parallel is that of King David whose dreadful fall into sin does not mean we refuse to read his psalms.

Luther was also impatient with the Anabaptists, some of whom behaved in an absurd fashion. Anabaptists were correct in their view of the gathered church but persecution hindered them from the opportunity to develop as outstanding theologians. We do well to remember that like all of us Luther had clay feet. He was a child of his times. The marvel is that amazing achievements came by him through God's power and grace.

Luther was primarily a seminary professor from 1512 onwards to the end of his life in 1546. Yet at the same time he was an outstanding pastor and preacher, as we will see. Theology is the engine which drives all true gospel work. Luther was a formidable theologian. He used this gift to recover several primary issues, including the crucial doctrine of salvation. I will outline the principal legacy that Martin Luther left to the universal Church, namely justification by faith. Luther, like all humans, had feet of clay. As indicated above, he had significant faults and these I will consider under a final heading which is 'Luther and reformation of denominations today'.

A sketch of Luther's life

Martin Luther was born in Eisleben in 1483. His parents were deeply religious and hard working. Hans Luther worked in the copper mining industry. He was never rich but he spent what he could on the education of his children.

Luther was well prepared for the work to which he was called. He earned the best academic credentials the medieval German Church could confer. Universities were not established in the German Empire until the middle of the fourteenth century: Prague (1348), Vienna (1305), Heidelberg (1368), Cologne (1388), Erfurt (1392) and Leipzig (1409).[1] Frederick the Wise established a new university in Wittenberg in 1502 which Luther would cause to become famous. Hans Luther wanted Martin to become a lawyer and paid for him to become a student at the Erfurt University in 1501. He studied for his MA which he achieved in the shortest possible time, graduating with excellence and coming second out of seventeen.

It was during July of 1505 that Martin was caught in a thunderstorm. He was terrified that he would be killed by a lightning strike which in fact killed a friend who was with him in that storm. He vowed that he would become a monk. His parents were deeply disappointed by his decision. Hans Luther was outraged and disowned Martin, although was later reconciled. Martin entered an Augustinian monastery in Erfurt, August 1505, at the age of twenty-one. He was ordained priest in 1507.

In Erfurt the Augustinian monks had established a general course of studies for their members. As a doctor of theology the respective chair had to fill the professorship of theology at the university as well. Through the works of Gabriel Biel, also Ockham, Duns Scotus, Petrus of Ailly and Thomas Aquinas, Martin was introduced to Christian dogmatics. Augustine was the most important theologian for Martin. It was largely through Augustine that he perceived the limitations of the scholastic scholars such as Aquinas. At that time Johannes von Staupitz was vicar general of the German Augustinian monasteries. He wished to free himself from the responsibility and it was obvious he prepared Luther to be his successor. Under his spiritual guidance Luther graduated through all levels of theological study up to and including his doctorate — and this within the shortest possible time frame. Five years of study was the minimum requirement.

All this took place in spite of the fact that Martin was in spiritual turmoil. He was tormented because he had no assurance of salvation. He tried everything, including fasting and confession of all known sin. In 1513 he began lecturing on the Psalms. He went on to expound Romans and then Galatians and Hebrews. This intense study of the Scriptures was the means of his conversion. He wrestled with the meaning of the word 'righteousness' in Psalm 31 and followed that up by studying the New Testament equivalent in Romans 1:17. When he saw that God's righteousness is a free gift received by faith he was instantly liberated. He declared: 'Thereupon I felt myself to be reborn and to have gone through open doors into paradise.'[2]

The first of the three principal events of the Reformation was the posting of the ninety-five theses on the door of the Castle Church at Wittenberg in 1517. These theses were far-ranging and dealt with more than condemnation of the indulgence traffic of Johan Tetzel. For instance article 32 declares that the burning of heretics is contrary to the will of the Holy Spirit. In explanation Luther refers to the burning of John Huss and Jerome at the Council of Constance. He upholds these brave believers as good Christians who were burned unjustly as heretics, apostates and antichristian. Luther also condemned the burning of the martyr Savonarola by Pope Alexander VI (1492–1503). It is important to understand that the indulgences did not concern eternal life. That was not the issue. Indulgences were sold to shorten time spent in purgatory. These could be bought for oneself or for one's relatives. This was made clear by Tetzel as we can soon see from the kind of appeal he made in his sales technique:

'Listen to the voices of your dear dead relatives and friends, beseeching you and saying, "Pity us, pity us. We are in dire torment from which you can redeem us for a pittance." Do you not wish to? Open your ears. Hear the father saying to his son, the mother to her daughter, "We bore you, brought you up, left you our fortunes, and you are so cruel and hard that you are not willing for so little to set us free. Will you let us lie here in flames? Will you delay our promised glory?" Remember that you are able to release them, for,

> *"As soon as the coin in the coffer rings,*
> *The soul from purgatory springs."'*

Martin felt deep indignation about this fraudulent practice. He seethed inside. This anger was evident in the ninety-five theses. The speed at which the theses were distributed is one of the wonders of church history. The devoted scholar Myconius suggested that 'within two weeks all of Germany, and inside a month, all of Christianity had read his theses as though the angels themselves carried the message'. Almost immediately an electric excitement framed popular reactions. Luther's reformation had begun with an air of the supernatural about it. His instant impact on German ecclesiastical and political life seemed miraculous.[3]

One outcome was the drying up of the income that was generated by the indulgence sales. Martin said he would 'knock a hole in Tetzel's drum'. Soon Tetzel was unable to appear on the streets for fear of being attacked by a mob and hanged. The indulgence scandal wore Tetzel down. Within a year he lay dying. Luther alone of all men wrote to comfort him, suggesting that he should not take the whole blame for the indulgence traffic upon himself.

The Pope's efforts to silence Luther were systematic. He was motivated by the fact that the ninety-five theses had a devastating effect on the money-raising efforts of the Vatican. The Pope asked for the leaders of the Augustinians to deal with Luther. Accordingly he was summoned to Heidelberg where he presented a powerful theological case for the ninety-five theses. Clearly discipline was not forthcoming from his fellow-Augustinians.

Luther was summoned to appear at Rome to answer for his writings. But Prince Frederick intervened on his behalf and secured a hearing for Luther in the presence of Cardinal Cajetan in Augsburg. This resulted in a fierce clash and exhausted the patience of the Cardinal. Luther's life was saved narrowly at this point. He was informed that there was a warrant for his arrest and he would be taken to Rome. It is certain that he would never have survived that. A faithful servant aroused Luther in the middle of the night and he made a quick escape through a back gate of the city, followed by a forty-minute non-stop journey by horse to reach Monheim. On the way home he saw copies of the orders to the Cardinal authorizing his arrest. We admire the providential way in which his life was preserved from execution. Many expected that he would soon be burned as John Huss was, a hundred years earlier.

The next step to silence Luther was to call him to a public debate with Johann Eck, the champion Romish debater of the time. This clearly was designed to intimidate Luther. The disputation took place in Leipzig in 1519. To the immense pleasure of the opponents of Luther, Eck seemed invincible. He seemed to have the upper hand in the first debates which were with Karlstadt, Luther's companion. It was a different matter when he faced Luther, who refuted Eck's arguments clearly. When Eck realized that Luther was winning the debate he resorted to the desperate measure of intimidation, labelling Luther a heretic who was following in the footsteps of John Huss and who deserved the same treatment as that heretic. Luther said that he did agree with Huss. This was courageous and was admired by the younger humanists who rallied to his support.[4]

The second principal event in this crucial period took place in 1520 and this was Luther's response to his excommunication from the Church of Rome. He was deeply shocked by this because he had hoped and prayed that his exposure of corruption and call for reformation would be taken seriously. The bull of excommunication was published everywhere, to discourage people from reading Luther's works. Luther's reaction was to call together the faculty and students of Wittenberg University and to organize a procession to march through the streets and then out through the gate of the city where the rubbish was taken to be burned. He had ordered that a large bonfire be prepared. When the procession arrived, they gathered round the bonfire. Luther ordered that all the books of papal law which had kept so many in bondage for so long be thrown into the flames. When this was done Luther drew from his coat the papal bull of excommunication and threw it into the fire.

This action was a signal that the people should cast away the bondage of papal law and be free.

The news of Luther's daring action and of his contempt for Romish tradition spread everywhere. It served to bring courage to all those who supported the Reformation. In his biography Richard Friedenthal expresses the significance of this action well:

> In an act so radical as to be unparalleled he first, and far more significantly, burned the decretals, the foundation of the papacy and the institutional Church. His contemporaries rightly regarded this as his most daring action; the burning of the bull was secondary, and is not even mentioned in the reports. Luther's burning of the entire body of law built up through the centuries meant the end of the medieval ascendancy of the Church, which saw itself embodied in this collection of statutes. It also meant divorce from Rome, and not merely from the Curia and the papacy. The canon law had

grown out of the Latin thought of ancient Rome, out of the
tradition of the Roman emperors; it was the continuation of
imperial Rome, whose heritage the Church had assumed.[5]

Eleander, the papal nuncio, reported to Rome the difficulty he
encountered when he sought to enforce the excommunication and
the ban on reading Luther's books. He reported that nine-tenths
of the Germans cried, 'Luther!' and the other tenth, 'Death to the
Pope!'[6]

The third and final act of this dramatic time took place the
following year in the city of Worms. Luther was required to appear
before Emperor Charles V and publicly renounce his writings. This
was designed to frighten him into submission. How could one man
defy the Pope, the Emperor and 1000 years of tradition? Before
the imperial gathering Luther stood his ground. About twenty of
his books were exhibited on a table in the packed auditorium, and
he was called on to renounce them. He argued that if his writings
were biblical, and he believed that they were, then he could not
renounce them.

The drama of this historic occasion is captured well by Bainton
when he describes the scene as follows:

Eck to Luther, 'Martin, you have not sufficiently distinguished
your works. The earlier were bad and the latter worse. Your
plea to be heard from Scripture is the one always made by
heretics. You do nothing but renew the errors of Wyclif and
Huss. How will the Jews, how will the Turks, exult to hear
Christians discussing whether they have been wrong all these
years! Would you put your judgment above that of so many
famous men and claim that you know more than they all?
You have no right to call into question the most holy orthodox
faith, instituted by Christ the perfect lawgiver, proclaimed

throughout the world by the apostles, sealed by the red blood of the martyrs, confirmed by the sacred councils, defined by the Church in which all our fathers believed until death and gave us inheritance, and which now we are forbidden by the pope and fathers to discuss lest there be no end of debate. I ask you, Martin — answer candidly and without horns — do you or do you not repudiate your books and the errors which they contain?'

Luther replied, 'Since your majesty and your lordships desire a simple reply, I will answer without horns and without teeth. Unless I am convicted by Scripture and plain reason — I do not accept the authority of popes and councils, for they have contradicted each other — my conscience is captive to the Word of God. I cannot and will not recant anything, for to go against conscience is neither right nor safe. God help me. Amen.'

The earliest version added the words: 'Here I stand, I cannot do otherwise.'[7]

From that momentous occasion we treasure the famous words of the Reformer.

'I cannot and will not recant anything, for to go against conscience is neither right nor safe. Here I stand, I cannot do otherwise. God help me. Amen.'

Historians argue about exactly what was said but whatever the details the outcome was certain. Luther rejected compromise.

The German princes were determined to protect Luther. In order to ensure his safekeeping, they arranged for him to be 'kidnapped' on his way home from the city of Worms. He was then taken to the Wartburg Castle, where he stayed, working relentlessly on his manuscripts until the storm had passed. His labour in the time spent at the Wartburg, which he called his 'Patmos', included the translation of the entire New Testament into his mother tongue.

The principal work of the Reformation had been achieved. From now on, it was a matter of consolidation.

In 1525 Martin married an ex-nun, Katherine von Bora. Two years earlier Luther had been involved in organizing the escape of twelve nuns from a nunnery. Katie was one of them. The couple were provided with a large house and property rather like a small farm which Katie managed very well. Hospitality had to be provided constantly for students and for a stream of visitors from all over Europe.

Katie was just the type of wife Luther needed. She was a conscientious mother, an efficient housekeeper, a wise manager of the farms, gardens, cattle and other livestock for which Luther had so little time. After 1540 he occasionally called her the 'boss of Zulsdorf', for sometimes she made lengthy visits to the farm which Luther had purchased when her brother was about to lose it through foreclosure. Katie's management must have added considerably to Luther's income, making it easier to provide for his family and some dozen nieces, nephews, aunts and needy relatives, and also freed Luther from many family details and responsibilities.

As noted earlier, Luther continued as a professor in the university, teaching the Bible and theology until his death at the age of sixty-two. Seminary work formed his basic source of income. To meet the urgent needs of reform Martin wrote in a prolific style. The printers were always eagerly awaiting his next manuscript. Eventually thirty publishers were established in Wittenberg. The output was so great during the tense Reformation period from 1517 to 1524 that it has never been exceeded subsequently in Germany. The quality of his work did not decline.

For instance in 1520 he wrote a treatise on good works based on the Ten Commandments, and on the papacy in which he described the Pope as 'the real antichrist of whom all the Scripture speaks'. In a further work on Rome with the title *The Address to the German Nobility* Luther disallowed the authority of the Pope over civil governments and expounded the truth of the priesthood of all believers. In this work he exposed the corruption of the Curia. Also in that year he wrote *The Babylonian Captivity of the Church* in which he reduced the number of the sacraments from seven to two. The Reformation brought about a completely new way of thinking and of life. Expositions and guidelines based on Scripture were needed on a wide variety of subjects. Fellow-reformers likened Luther to a modern Elijah.[8] In 1561 fellow German Cyriakis Spangenberg published a work in which he extolled Luther's writings as 'a treasure given by God, to be held in honour next to the Holy Bible' for Luther had 'set forth our dear Christ and the true way to heaven on every occasion'. Spangenberg recognized the clarity and power of Luther's writings declaring:

> *No other teacher has ever given clearer and more understandable instruction regarding the proper distinction of law and gospel, and with it a correct understanding of righteousness, good works and repentance.*[9]

On his way to settle a dispute that had broken out in Mansfield, Luther was taken ill. He died in Mansfield. His body was taken back to be buried in the church in Wittenberg, the same church where he had nailed the ninety-five theses. Luther never accumulated money and Katherine was left with very little. Thankfully the Elector made a provision for her. She died six years later.

Luther as pastor

In his essay on Luther and modern church history James M. Kittelson refutes the idea that reformation of the Church was the driving force in Luther's personal development and in his career as monk, professor, theologian and even reformer. Kittelson suggests that his care of souls is the dynamic by which one can understand both his life and his works.[10]

There are five spheres in which we note the function of Luther as pastor. The first is in his care for his own family. He and Katie had six children of their own, three sons and three daughters. One daughter died in infancy and Magdalena died aged about eleven. In the wider family that became part of this very large family were two daughters and four sons of a sister of Luther; Hans Polner, son of another sister; and another sister; and another nephew, the son of his brother; a great-niece, Anna Strauss; a lady teacher, Margarethe von Mochau; other tutors of the Luther children, at one time numbering six, and Aunt Lena, the same aunt who had escaped with Katie from the nunnery and who faithfully cared for the children until her death in 1537. To these more or less permanent members of the family must be added the numerous nuns and monks who found themselves without occupation, the twelve table companions who spent varying lengths of time under the Luther roof, a steady flow of guests, and indigent pastors without pulpits. All who for any length of time took up their abode in the Luther house were considered members of the family and were expected to conform to the family customs. They were expected to study the Catechism, pray, and attend the family devotions, which included the reading from a family systematic teaching devotional on Sundays.

There was also provision for wholesome recreation in the Luther family life. A bowling lane in Luther's garden was much enjoyed by the young people and friends of the family. Sometime Luther himself found time to roll a few balls. The children had ample space for play in the roomy grounds of the Luther House. Music and singing were enjoyed by the family, and chess was a game much enjoyed by Luther. Time at the meal table gave Martin the opportunity to relate to his family, to visitors and to students who would often write down his sayings which were later published as his *Table Talk*. His sense of humour was often present. For instance he marvelled at how one collector of relics had managed to collect a feather from the angel Gabriel! He was surprised that there were eighteen claimed burial places of Christ's apostles in Germany when our Lord had only appointed twelve!

Martin was a master of Christology and loved the book of Hebrews. He adored the incarnation as we see in this composition:

Our little Lord, we give thee praise
That thou hast designed to take our ways.
Born of a maid a man to be,
And all the angels sing to thee.

The eternal Father's Son he lay
Cradled in a crib of hay.
The everlasting God appears
In our frail flesh and blood and tears.

What the globe could not unwrap
Nestled lies in Mary's lap.
Just a baby, very wee,
Yet Lord of all the world is he.

The second sphere of shepherding or caring concerned Luther's fellow-tutors in the university. The impact made by Luther on his fellow professors at the University of Wittenberg was immense. He did not rest until he had persuaded all twenty-two professors of the biblical truths upon which the Reformation was grounded. The entire faculty supported Martin through the most critical period of peril from 1517 to 1522 when he was excommunicated and his writings were banned. Bonds of attachment were close. For example Melanchthon said, 'If there is anyone on earth I love it is Martin and his pious writings. Never was there a greater man on the face of the earth. I would rather die than sever myself from that man.'[11] Nicholas von Amsdorf was another who turned from scholastic theology to become an ardent advocate of the Reformation. His closeness to Martin is seen in the fact that he travelled with him to the City of Worms and was at his side when he was kidnapped and spirited away to the Wartburg.

The third sphere of Luther's pastoral care involved his students. An examination of old records reveals that no fewer than 16,992 students enrolled at the University of Wittenberg between 1520 and 1560. Most came from Germany but some from England, France, Poland and Scandinavia. For instance two students from Sweden, Olaus and Lurentius Petri who trained under Luther, became preachers of unusual energy and effectiveness. They were instrumental in turning the whole of their native country of Sweden from the Papacy to the Protestantism of the Bible.[12]

The fourth sphere of pastoral care concerned the people of Wittenberg who attended the Castle Church. We will see this as we view his preaching ministry there.

The fifth area of shepherding concerned Luther's function as prior in charge of eleven Augustinian monasteries from May 1512. This oversight demanded much pastoral care and correspondence. In one instance he had to dismiss Father Michael Dressel from his leadership role in the monastery at Neustadt for failing to keep peace and unity. This came after he had previously been exhorted in a most fraternal way by Luther to establish unity.[13] Eventually the monasteries and convents for nuns would empty as the incumbents sought normal Christian employment.

Luther as preacher

Luther shared the preaching at the Castle Church in Wittenberg with John Bugenhagen, his close friend and colleague who occupied the position of town pastor and professor in the university. Bugenhagen was often absent as he promoted the reformation in northern Germany and in Denmark. Some years Martin preached 180 times. In 1522 it was fewer at 46, in 1530, as we will see, about 40 times, and in 1540 just 43. Of the approximately 4000 sermons he preached, about 2,300 have been preserved in some form. His preaching must be set within the context of all his other labours including seminary lectures, writing treatises, mentoring students, correspondence and attending conferences. It is a wonder he did not suffer from what we today call 'burnout'.

Meuser on Luther as a preacher of the Word observes:

> *For Luther, preaching was not a preacher's ideas stimulated by the prod of a text. It was the preacher's reflection about God and life. Christian preaching, when it is faithful to the Word of God in the Scriptures about our need and God's response to it, is God speaking. In the teaching and exhortation, he was faithful to the Word of God. When it presents Christ, faith becomes possible, it is God speaking. It is God's very own audible address to all who hear it, just as surely as if Christ had spoken it.*
>
> *Though Luther often said that a sermon is simply composed of teaching and exhortation, he did not preach in that way.*

He preached as if the sermon were not for a classroom but a battleground! Every sermon was a battle for the souls of the people, an apocalyptic event that set the doors of heaven and hell in motion, part of the continuing conflict between the Lord and Satan. The Word is God's sword in this cosmic warfare through which the power of Christ invades life today.

The sermon itself is, therefore, a saving event. When God speaks, things can never be the same again. God's Word touches the hearer, condemns, offers forgiveness, appeals and draws. No one can listen in cool detachment on the perimeter in a neutral stance. One cannot go away from preaching in the same relationship as before. Neutrality means that the devil has won the skirmish. When the Word about Christ is preached, God has spoken and one answers yes or no. There is no alternative.[14]

With standards that he set himself like this it is not surprising that he was prone to discouragement. In 1530 he was disconsolate because he felt there was no progress in the sanctification of the congregation. From January 1530 to September he preached only three times and two of those were by the express command of the Prince. He often used hyperbole to express himself and this time he declared that had he known in advance what a miserable calling preaching was, then twenty-four horses could not have been enough to have drawn him into it! He viewed preaching as hard work and described it as 'a rotten office, whose misery is such that a person would rather be a swineherd!' In 1528 he warned the congregation at the Castle Church that he would stop preaching unless he saw more fruit for the gospel. In his New Year sermon in 1530 he complained bitterly of their selfishness. A short time later he said he would rather preach to raving dogs than to them and that from then on he would confine himself to the classroom. It appears that he was refreshed by a stay (holiday) at Coburg and suddenly without any apology or explanation he resumed preaching in September 1530, and in 1531 he was back to his average of 180 sermons a year.[15]

In his preaching Luther was popular and very direct in his style. He enjoyed a natural mastery of language and he taught preachers of the Reformation to preach in the language of the people. Martin was gifted in his ability to convey profound theology and devotion. He was subject to the standard training in rhetoric which was part of the university education of the late Middle Ages. Today we call this subject homiletics. Ulrich Nembach has shown that:

> Luther learned from the literary studies of the Renaissance to look at the traditional textbooks on rhetoric with a certain objectivity. He was critical of both Aristotle and Augustine. Quintilian, on the other hand, was very popular with Luther, and a good teacher for him to follow. He taught Luther a rhetoric appropriate for a teacher who aimed at showing his listeners how to live a good life. Among the Roman orators, Quintilian was relatively free of the affectations one usually associates with classical rhetoric, and, as Luther well understood, a preacher of the gospel has to get beyond rhetoric, as helpful as it may be.[16]

There is a wonderful account of the effect of Luther's preaching as he made his journey to the city of Worms to stand trial before Emperor Charles V and the panoply of the Roman Catholic Church. By this time at all levels of German society his was a prophetic voice. He was a hero. The smouldering antagonism between Rome and the German lands had been ignited into a fire which burned with fury. Shopkeepers, students, housewives, poets, peasants and princes discussed the implications of what this monk had written and wondered what the outcome would be. On his way to Worms Luther stayed over at the university he knew so well. He was asked to preach on the text for the day which was John 20:19-31, which he did. Eoban Hess, a professor of the university at Erfurt, described the effects on the hearers of this sermon thus: 'By the power of his mouth, hearts were melted like snow by the breath of spring as he showed the way to heaven's goods which had been closed for centuries.' This sermon was published seven times that year.[17]

The description 'hearts were melted like snow by the breath of spring' is a vivid reminder of what preaching is all about. It is not merely the conveying of information for the mind. Yes, preaching must be exposition of the Word of God but the purpose is more than the provision of information. The aim is to move hearts to repentance and to holiness of life. The preacher addresses hearers in the wholeness of their being. An overhead projector can convey information but does not have a personality like a gospel preacher has, through which the truth is applied to the consciences of men and women, boys and girls.

In addition to books a steady stream of tracts was published. These were illustrated by gifted artists and made a powerful visual impact. Lucas Cranach was a famous artist in Wittenberg. Unlike many artists he was wealthy. The number of tracts published in Germany for the period 1521 to 1524 exceeds the quantity for any other four years in German history up to the present.

Luther as theologian

The foundational principles recovered by the Reformation are always relevant for all pastors. Three most basic principles are *sola Scriptura* (Scripture alone), *sola fide* (by faith alone), and *sola gratia* (by grace alone).

That God's Word comes to us in the form of a book was Luther's discovery. When grasped, that principle alone achieved the progress of the Reformation. Luther understood that the truth is vested in the Bible, not in a pope in Rome. Moreover the truth is not mediated through dreams or visions or the ecstasies of charismatics. There were fanatical charismatics in Luther's day. The Zwickau prophets arrived in Wittenberg when Luther was in hiding at the Wartburg Castle. They claimed to have special direct revelations from God. Sadly one of Luther's associates, Andreas Karlstadt, was carried away with this spirit of fanaticism. Melanchthon was unable to handle the confusion and declared: 'The dam is broken, and I cannot stem the waters.' Alarmed, the City Council called Luther back from the Wartburg to restore order. This was accomplished through the preaching of the Word. Luther resisted the Zwickau prophets and chided them saying that they had swallowed the Holy Ghost, feathers and all!

Sola Scriptura, Scripture alone, was the principle used to rid the Church of human doctrines. For instance, the sacraments had multiplied to seven. The sacramental system of Rome controlled the lives of members from birth to death. Luther examined these issues in the light of Scripture. He maintained that what is not sanctioned in the Word must be abandoned. Not only was false teaching to be rejected, but right practice was to be restored. An example is the withholding of the cup from communicants in the communion service. The New Testament teaches clearly that all believers should partake of the wine. A major issue was that of the relationship of Church and State. Nowhere in Scripture do we find warrant for the idea that the Church has authority over civil governments, yet Rome sought to exercise authority over kings and rulers.

There is power in Scripture because it carries with it the very mind and will of God and no human power or authority can withstand that. Luther resisted the authority of the papacy and of church councils on the basis that it could be shown clearly that they had erred and failed to conform to Scripture. *Sola Scriptura* was the sword by which the battle for truth was won. The Reformers examined the doctrines and practices of the Roman Catholic Church in the light of Scripture.

The effective reforming power of Scripture is wonderfully described by Luther in these words:

> *I simply taught, preached, wrote God's Word: otherwise I did nothing. And then, while I slept, or drank Wittenberg beer with my Philip or my Amsdorf, the Word so greatly weakened the Papacy that never a prince or emperor inflicted such damage upon it. I did nothing. The Word did it all. Had I desired to foment trouble, I could have brought great bloodshed upon Germany. Yea, I could have started such a little game at Worms, that the Emperor would not have been safe. But what would it have been? A mug's game. I left it to the Word.*[18]

The close personal friends referred to here were Philip Melanchthon and Nickolaus von Amsdorf. Martin's sense of humour and use of hyperbole shines brightly here since his prodigious work output was colossal and he did not have much time to spare.

A reformed church by its very nature calls for constant reform and conformity to the Word. The Reformation saying is *ecclesia reformata, ecclesia semper reformanda* — 'the reformed Church must be a Church which is always reforming itself'.

For instance the music that is used and the words used in the singing of hymns and choruses must be examined. What is superficial or unbiblical should be rejected. There is a wide choice of God-honouring material for singing which is true to Scripture which we can use. A further issue for reform is to adhere to biblical standards in the election of elders and deacons.

Immediately Luther came to salvation his preaching became biblical. Many pastors today preach an easy believism and need to reform their understanding of God's way of salvation. One way to bring about reform in this respect is to preach through the epistle to the Romans. That letter was the theological textbook of the reformation. The apostle Paul teaches that salvation is never attained by works of righteousness. Salvation is the free gift of God and is received by faith alone, *sola fide*. The basis of God's justification of the sinner is the imputed righteousness of Christ.

Is salvation by free will or is it by free grace?

This issue perplexes every generation of Christians. Erasmus was the champion of the Roman Catholic view on this subject. He held the doctrine of free will which is Roman Catholic doctrine. Erasmus was born in Holland, the illegitimate son of a Roman Catholic priest and a physician's daughter. Erasmus did more than any other scholar to revive classical studies. He also edited and published the Greek New Testament which both Tyndale and Luther used in their translations. Erasmus, in his writings, exposed the corruption of the clergy. He was popular with popes, kings and scholars. It seemed that he would side with the Reformation but he did not understand the subject of the free grace of God. In 1524 Erasmus attacked Luther's doctrine of total depravity in a book with the title *The Freedom of the Will*.

The free will idea can, and often does, lead to distorted views of God as though he is unable to change a sinner. Sometimes this distortion is twisted to the point where God is depicted as powerless before the will of the sinner.

Luther's answer to Erasmus appeared a year later in 1525. He called his book *The Bondage of the Will*. Some consider this to be his greatest work. Erasmus did not understand the core theological issue whereas Luther grasped the difference between human responsibility and human inability. Fallen man will always by nature choose his own way because his will is at enmity to God. By nature fallen man is not subject to the law of God (Rom. 8:7-8). Luther explained that it is necessary that the Holy Spirit give the new birth, as is clearly expressed by Paul in Ephesians 2:1-10.

'He interpreted sin in the Augustinian sense of a self-centredness which destroyed the capacity freely to will the good. The will is enslaved to the self and has no true spiritual freedom. This bondage of the will Luther saw as man's supreme spiritual danger, always binding him to himself and his own interests and blinding him to God and the needs of his brother man.' To Luther, unbelief was the fundamental sin.[19]

Luther's legacy — justification by faith alone

Martin Luther's principal legacy to the universal Church was the recovery of a clear doctrine of justification by faith. Of this truth Luther declared that it was the standing or falling doctrine of a church. If this truth is eliminated the church falls.

In his own experience Luther became a prototype of what it is to be saved by imputed righteousness. He fits perfectly into Romans chapter four. Abraham believed. Righteousness was imputed to him. He was saved without the works of the law. King David followed that pattern. So did Luther.

Today the teaching of N. T. Wright, formerly Bishop of Durham, contradicts Luther on justification by the imputed righteousness of Christ. This teaching is related to what is called 'The New Perspective on Paul'. Following theologians E. P. Sanders, Krister Stendahl and J. D. G. Dunn, N. T. Wright suggests that Luther misreads Paul. His view is that the Jews did believe in grace and did not follow the idea that salvation is by works. The two great obstacles to N. T. Wright are the letters of Paul to the Romans and the Galatians. There Paul sustains his case that the Jews were works-based. In Galatians Paul makes it plain that any addition of law-keeping whatsoever, whether circumcision or anything else, is to be rejected. Those who add to grace are under a curse (Gal. 1:8). Moreover Paul maintains a clear line which separates justification from sanctification.

Luther's commentary on Romans, which contains virtually the whole of the revolutionary theological thrust of the Reformation, having been buried in the Vatican Library, was not published until 1908. It is now volume 25 in the Concordia set of Luther's *Complete Works*. His understanding of law and grace is plainly stated and commentators since have not failed to follow Paul's sense — Charles Hodge (1835), Robert Haldane (1839), F. L. Godet (1879), J. B. Lightfoot (1895), Prof. John Murray (1959), Dr Martyn Lloyd-Jones (10 volumes 1985ff), Douglas Moo (1991). But the new perspective requires us to take a different direction. It seems that the doctrine of justification by faith will always be a target of Satan.

Martin Luther called imputed righteousness an alien righteousness; that is, it comes from the outside. It comes from God and is put around the believer. Say I received a garment made in China and I put it round me, it would be alien in that it comes from the outside. It is from another world. It is not of my making.

Here is a summary of facts about this alien righteousness which makes us acceptable before God and gives us a right to be in his family as sons and daughters.

1. This righteousness comes from God the Father. It is a gift.

2. This righteousness is put on us in an act of God the Father. It is an act, *not a process*. It is a once-and-for-all act never to be repeated. We do nothing. We believe and come into union with Christ by faith. But the receiving of the righteousness and the act of justification belong to God. We are passive. We do nothing but believe.

3. This righteousness consists of the complete and perfect life of Christ. It is the sum total of his obedience. He has done what we should have done. Jeremiah 23:6 sums the matter up: 'This is the name by which he will be called: The LORD Our Righteousness.'

4. This righteousness is given because of the atonement. God's Son is the propitiation. He is the burnt offering which satisfies the justice of God. This propitiation effectively removes the wrath of God from the sinner.

5. The imputation of this righteousness precedes justification. Note the order. Righteousness is imputed. Then justification follows as an act of the Father.

6. There is absolutely no merit in receiving this righteousness. I receive it not because I am obedient. I receive it through faith as an instrument and not through faith as a merit.

7. This righteousness is a human righteousness. We are human. Our sins emanate from our fallen sinful humanity. We are born with Adam's first sin imputed to us. We are born moreover with Adam's sinful nature. The righteousness which is the basis of our justification is the human obedience and human perfection of Christ. This human righteousness is put to our account.

8. This imputed righteousness leads us to a life of righteousness. We are justified out of faith (*ek pisteôs*) and then led to live a life

of faith (*eis pistin*) (Rom. 1:17) as it is written: 'He who through faith is righteous shall live' (RSV).

9. The righteousness imputed to us is never the same as the righteous life we live, and the righteous life we live is never the basis of our justification. Christ's perfect righteousness imputed to us is always and only the sole basis of our justification.

10. The righteousness which the Father imputes to us is external. It is legal. It has to do with justice. The righteous life implanted into believers by the Holy Spirit is an internal thing, is progressive and is never perfect in this life.

Luther and reformation of denominations today

By way of conclusion I will consider reformation today.

It is the responsibility of all pastors to aim at conformity to the Word of God in their own lives and in all the teaching and practice of the local church. Sometimes pastors are involved in an extensive reformation of the churches they lead. I know of one who was called to a church which was run by a committee. The membership stood at about sixty. He accepted the call on condition that he would be free to preach the reformed faith, establish an eldership and a diaconate, rewrite the constitution and base the church on a reformed confession of faith. All this took about five years. In the process the church grew to about ninety members. That is exceptional. Many independent churches are controlled by a power group, a diaconate, eldership, or a committee. Often the power group is held firmly in the grip of traditional practice with the result that there is hostility to change or reform. If a power group in an independent church comes to dislike their pastor we can be sure his days are numbered.

Martin Luther was unique because his faithfulness to Scripture and courageous stand for the gospel affected the whole future of Christ's Church on earth. Pastors of churches work in a tiny sphere by comparison. Nevertheless they often have their own demanding battles to fight.

Luther was not without his faults. He is accused of fracturing the unity of the Church. However it should be noted that in early history the Church divided into Roman Catholic and Eastern Orthodox denominations. Luther erred in the way he responded to Ulrich Zwingli. He was intolerant and so missed an opportunity to maintain unity. Later in his life he lost patience with the Jews. As we see from Romans chapters nine to eleven the Scriptures require that we maintain a loving attitude toward Jews. For centuries Roman Catholic leaders depicted Luther as a drunken, aggressive, unworthy character. It was in 1939 that Roman Catholic historian Joseph Lortz published his epochal work *The Reformation in Germany*. Up to that time it was the custom of the Roman Catholic Church to regard Luther as a heretic. Lortz challenged that idea and admitted that the blame lay with the leaders of the Church for not responding positively to Luther's call for reform. Other scholars have followed Lortz. A radical change has taken place in Catholic perceptions of Luther.[20]

The most encouraging feature of the sixteenth-century Reformation is that a vast change took place during a period of five years. 'Is anything too hard for me?' (Jer. 32:27). Could Reformation on that scale be repeated in the Roman Catholic Church today?

Is the Roman Catholic Church reformable? The answer is clearly no! The Council of Trent (1545–1563) was organized as a response to the Lutherans. It is estimated that a third of the Roman Catholic leaders at Trent were in favour of reform but they were overruled. The tragic outcome of the Council of Trent was the formulation of statements which are absurd and extravagant. Anathemas were pronounced at Trent condemning the doctrine of justification by faith alone. Curses were pronounced in writing on those who believe it. That was an appalling mistake. Rome boasts that she never changes. That precludes reform. When Roman Catholics embrace the biblical doctrine of justification by faith alone almost invariably they leave the Roman Catholic Church. This has taken place on a large scale in Roman Catholic Latin America. Large numbers have left and joined mostly Pentecostal churches.

Statistics show that Catholics are numerous in countries like Germany (19 million), the USA (46 million), the Philippines (38 million), Mexico (51 million), Colombia (20 million) and the Argentine (24 million). A large proportion of Catholics are nominal and seldom attend church.

The Anglican Church is a parallel with the Roman Catholic Church. In 1662 the Government passed a law called 'The Act of Uniformity' which was so drastic that it compelled all Anglican clergy to follow set forms of worship. This compelled about 2,000 English Puritans to leave the Established Church. Since that time the Church of England has been regarded as past reform. No leader or group of leaders has seriously attempted to reform the Church of England since 1662.

Another great area of possible return to the doctrines of Luther is within the Lutheran communities round the world. Sweden, Norway, Denmark and Finland have large Lutheran denominations. The Lutheran Church in Finland is much more evangelical than most national churches in Europe. There are 3.4 million Lutherans in the USA.

The decisive way in which the Lord intervened in the years 1517 to 1522 was an answer to prayer to devoted believers who cohered together in a movement known as the *Devotia Moderna*, the Brethren of the Common Life. That encourages us to prevail in prayer for global revival and for reformation to be advanced powerfully. I conclude with the benediction, 'Now to him who is able to do immeasurably more than all we ask or imagine, according to his power that is at work within us, to him be glory in the church and in Christ Jesus throughout all generations, for ever and ever! Amen' (Eph. 3:20-21).

SELECT BIBLIOGRAPHY

A nine-page select bibliography including a page of website locations is found in *Essays on Martin Luther* edited by Donald K. McKim, Cambridge University Press, 2003. Since he captures the time so well, Roland Bainton deserves his place as having written the most popular biography of Luther with the title *Here I Stand*. The Lion Paperback, 412 pages edition, was published in 1983. A note says that over one million copies had been sold. My favourite biography is by the German, E. G. Schwiebert, *Luther and his Times*, Concordia, 1950. I value Richard Friedenthal's biography published by Weidenfeld and Nicholson in 1970, but this work, as far as I know, is out of print. Also out of print is the excellent work of James Atkinson, *Martin Luther and the birth of Protestantism*, M M and S, 352 pages, 1968. Commended is Bernard Lohse, *Martin Luther; An Introduction to his Life and Work*, T. and T. Clark, 1987, and James M. Kittelson, *Luther the Reformer*, Augsburg, 1986. Those who read German will value Gerhard Ebeling, *Lutherstudien*, 5 vols, Tübingen.

5

William Perkins

Application in preaching

William Perkins (1558–1602) laboured with remarkable success at Cambridge which in its day was the leading centre for training Puritan divines. In him combined unusual spiritual qualities and ministerial skills. His youth was given to recklessness, profanity and drunkenness. While a student Perkins experienced a powerful conversion. This, it is believed, began when he overheard a woman in the street. She was chiding her naughty child and threatened to hand him over for punishment to 'drunken Perkins'! Perkins experienced a deep conviction and gave up his evil life. He also gave up the study of mathematics and his fascination with black magic and the occult, and took up theology. He joined Laurence Chaderton (1536–1640), his personal tutor and lifelong friend who Patrick Collinson has called 'the pope of Cambridge Puritanism'. Perkins became part of the spiritual brotherhood which was the foundation out of which Puritanism developed during the reign of Queen Elizabeth (1558–1602). Among the best-known leaders of that movement were Richard Greenham (1531–1591) and Richard Rogers (1550–1620). Perkins earned a bachelor's degree in 1581 and a master's degree in 1584.

WILLIAM PERKINS.

William Perkins

From 1584 until his death Perkins served as lecturer, or preacher, at Great St Andrew's Church, Cambridge. This most influential church was situated just across the street from Christ's College. St Andrew's was regularly packed with eager hearers, many of whom were converted under Perkins' ministry. He also served as a Fellow at Christ's College from 1584 to 1595. Fellows were required to preach, lecture and tutor students and also work as 'guides to learning as well as guardians of finances, morals, and manners'. Perkins served the university in several capacities. He was Dean of Christ's College from 1590 to 1591. He catechized the students at Corpus Christi College on Thursday afternoons, lecturing on the Ten Commandments in a manner that deeply impressed the students. On Sunday afternoons he worked as an adviser, counselling the spiritually distressed.

Perkins was a powerful preacher. His aim was to reach and minister to the spiritual needs of a wide range of hearers. He spent as much time on exegesis of the text as he did prayerfully considering the spiritual state of his hearers. He ministered to the prisoners at Cambridge jail including those who were on death row. Samuel Clarke provides a striking example of Perkins' pastoral care. He says a condemned prisoner was climbing the gallows, looking 'half-dead', when Perkins said to him, 'What man! What is the matter with thee? Art thou afraid of death?' The prisoner confessed that he was less afraid of death than of what would follow it. 'Sayest thou so,' said Perkins. 'Come down again, man, and thou shalt see what God's grace will do to strengthen thee.' When the prisoner came down, they knelt together, hand in hand, and Perkins offered 'such an effectual prayer in confession of sins … as made the poor prisoner burst out into abundance of tears'. Convinced the prisoner was brought 'low enough, even to hell's gates', Perkins showed him the freeness of the gospel in prayer. Clarke writes that the prisoner's eyes were opened 'to see how the black lines of all his sins were crossed, and cancelled with the red lines of his crucified

Saviour's precious blood; so graciously applying it to his wounded conscience, as made him break out into new showers of tears for joy of the inward consolation which he found'. The prisoner arose from his knees, went cheerfully up the ladder, testified of salvation in Christ's blood, and bore his death with patience, 'as if he actually saw himself delivered from the hell which he feared before, and heaven opened for the receiving of his soul, to the great rejoicing of the beholders'.

Fuller writes that Perkins' sermons were of many colours: 'They seemed to be "all law and all gospel, all cordials and all corrosives, as the different necessities of people apprehended" them.' He was able to reach many types of people in various classes, being systematic, scholarly, solid and simple at the same time. Most important is the fact that he lived his sermons. What he declared in the pulpit he was in daily life.

Perkins pioneered Puritan casuistry — the art of dealing with 'cases of conscience' by self-examination and scriptural diagnosis.

It is no exaggeration to say that William Perkins as a theologian and pastor became the main architect of the Puritan movement in his generation. He was handicapped in his right hand and so wrote with his left. Fuller said of him, 'This Ehud, with a left-handed pen did stab the Romish cause!'

As an author he was used to an astonishing degree. In his paper on Perkins at the Westminster Conference at Westminster Chapel in London in 2004, Joel Beeke asserted that 'Perkins was the first theologian to be more widely published in England than Calvin, and the first English Protestant theologian to have a major impact in the British Isles, on the European continent, and in North America. Many Puritan scholars marvel that Perkins' rare works have been largely unavailable until now.'

After his death his works were published eleven times up to 1635. These contained nearly fifty treatises. Joel Beeke researched the fact that at least fifty editions of Perkins' works were printed in Switzerland and in various parts of Germany. 'His writings were also translated into Spanish, French, Italian, Irish, Welsh, Hungarian and Czech.' In New England nearly one hundred Cambridge men who led early migrations, including William Brewster of Plymouth, Thomas Hooker of Connecticut, John Winthrop of Massachusetts Bay, and Roger Williams of Rhode Island, grew up in Perkins' shadow. Richard Mather was converted while reading Perkins' books. A century later Jonathan Edwards was fond of reading Perkins.

Perkins died in 1602 from kidney stones at the relatively young age of forty-four. His wife of seven years was pregnant at the time and caring for three small children.

His major writings include expositions of Galatians 1-5; Matthew 5-7; Hebrews 11; Jude; and Revelation 1-3; as well as treatises on predestination, the order of salvation, assurance of faith, the *Apostles' Creed*, the Lord's Prayer, the worship of God, the Christian life and vocation, ministry and preaching, the errors of Roman Catholicism and various cases of conscience.

We will concentrate now on Perkins' book on preaching. It is called *The Art of Prophesying*.

The Art of Prophesying

As far as I can tell, this was the first book on preaching within the three generations of English Puritans in the period 1558 to 1662. *The Art of Prophesying* was first published in Latin in 1592 and translated into English in 1606, four years after Perkins' death. In

1996 the Banner of Truth published a revised edition in modern English. In the twenty-first century the title is likely to convey the idea of a special charismatic gift of prophesying. That is not what Perkins meant. All the Puritan ministers believed that the apostolic period was unique and were cessationist; that is, they believed that charismatic gifts of tongues and prophesying direct from God had ceased and that churches are to be built up through preaching and teaching. Perkins took prophesying to mean the declaration of the Word of God through preaching. He also took it to mean praying on behalf of the congregation. It is the norm to understand a prophet to be one who speaks to the people from God and a priest as one who prays to God on behalf of the people. All believers are priests in the sense that they pray to God for each other. Perkins believed that public prayer in worship was vital and that it required preparation. He suggested that the public prayer be taken by the pastor or by a leader or officer in the church spiritually equipped for that responsibility. He advocated that public prayer should begin with confession of sin. He summarizes as follows: 'There are three elements in praying: (i) Carefully thinking about appropriate content in prayer; (ii) Setting the themes in an appropriate order; (iii) Expressing the prayer so that it is made in public in a way that is edifying for the congregation.'

Helpful guidelines for pastors

In *The Art of Prophesying* Perkins proceeds from the general to the particular. He begins with explaining the nature of the Bible as the Word of God. He outlines the canon of Scripture, and explains the principles for expounding Scripture. For instance, he addresses the subject of the physical body of Christ which is just as relevant today as it was then, since it is a subject which divides Protestants from Roman Catholics.

How do we understand the words, 'This is my body which is broken for you' (1 Cor. 11:24, NKJV)? Various interpretations have been given to this statement including: that the bread in the communion is actually the body of Christ, becoming so by conversion (the Roman Catholic view); or that the body of Christ is in, under, or with the bread (the Lutheran view). But to expound these words in either of these senses would be to disagree with a fundamental article of the faith: Christ 'ascended into heaven', and also with the nature of the sacrament, as a memorial of the absent body of Christ. Consequently another interpretation must be sought.

A different interpretation is that in this context the bread is a sign of the body. In this case the figure of speech known as metonymy is being employed — the name of one thing is used for something else which is related to it. This is an appropriate exposition for the following reasons:

First of all, it agrees with the analogy of faith in two ways:

1. 'He ascended into heaven'; he was taken up locally and visibly from the earth into heaven. Consequently his body is not to be received with the mouth at the communion, but by faith apprehending it in heaven.

2. He was 'born of the virgin Mary'; Christ had a true and natural body which was long, broad, firm, and seated and circumscribed in one particular place. If this is so, the bread in the Supper cannot be his actual body but must be only a sign or pledge of it.

On memorizing the sermon

The subject of preparation, the writing out of a sermon and whether the preacher should preach from rough notes or read his manuscript is often discussed. Perkins was clearly in favour of the discipline of writing out material but once the preparation was made he was in favour of freedom, 'There is no need to be overly anxious about the precise words we will use. As Horace says, words "will not unwillingly follow the matter that is premeditated".' Perkins was clearly in favour of using a rough outline and proceeding extempore from there for the sake of gaining Spirit-given unction. He warns against the preacher losing his way in a discourse which is embarrassing for both preacher and congregation. When men start off in the ministry they find it necessary to write out their materials and then follow an outline, but with more experience and a trained memory they are able to preach freely with just a rough outline. Very few have the confidence and an able memory to allow them to discard notes altogether.

On avoiding unnecessary controversy

Perkins gave sound advice about controversy. He exhorts as follows:

> *Reprove only the errors which currently trouble the church. Leave others alone if they lie dead in past history, or if they are not relevant to the people, unless you know that spiritual danger may still arise from them. This is the situation described in Revelation chapter two when the church at Pergamos was warned to beware of the Nicolaitans whose teaching had already influenced some of them.*

The necessity of a calling to the ministry

Perkins held firmly to the necessity of a call to the ministry which is the position expounded by Martin Holdt. Over a third of his book is devoted to the call of the minister. He opens up the subject by expounding Isaiah chapter six.

The manner in which Perkins divides the text is typical of the Puritans. The spiritual application which follows goes to the very heart of the calling of a pastor. Here is how Perkins hits the mark.

Isaiah's fear and amazement are described in two ways.

1. By two signs:
    i) A note of exclamation, 'Woe is me.'
    ii) A note of extreme dejection about himself, 'I am undone.'

2. By its two causes:
    i) He was an unclean man, and dwelt among unclean people.
    ii) He had seen the Lord. 'So I said: "Woe is me, for I am undone!"'

Perkins is careful to explain that Isaiah's confession of sin is referring not to some scandalous or outrageous sin but rather general unworthiness felt in the presence of the perfect holiness and majesty of God and suggests that 'a small fault in other men is a great one in ministers, and what may be to a certain extent pardonable in other men is not so in them'.

His exposition runs like this:

> The first point to note is the fear and sense of ecstasy into which the Lord drove his holy prophet, not in his anger against him but in his love for him; not as a punishment for his sin, but as an evidence of his further love. For the purpose of God in striking this fear into him was to enable him to be a true prophet, and a suitable messenger for himself.

> This may seem to be an unusual course for God to take in order to confirm and energise his servant in zeal and courage; to strike him with extreme fear, indeed to astonish and amaze

him. Yet it is clear that this is the way the Lord takes. It teaches us that all true ministers, especially those appointed to speak the greatest words in his church, must be first of all marked by a great sense of fear. They represent him and bring his message. The more afraid they are and the more they shrink under the contemplation of God's majesty and their own weakness, the more likely it is that they are truly called of God and appointed for worthy purposes in his church. Anyone who steps into this function without fear puts himself forward, but it is doubtful whether he is called by God as the prophet Isaiah clearly was.

Nor is such fear limited to Isaiah. Whenever God called any of his servants to any great work, he first drove them into this sense of fear and amazement. That is evident in Moses (Exod. 3:11), Jeremiah (Jer. 1:6), Paul (Acts 9:5) and others. The reason for this is clear; man's nature is always ready to take too much upon itself. God therefore in his wisdom puts a bridle into the corrupt nature of man and stuns him, lest he presume too much and trust himself too much.

In addition, a minister must teach his people to fear and reverence the Lord. But how can he teach others when he has not tied that bond in his own conscience and has never been cast down in admiration of God's glory and majesty?

Perkins concludes with the observation: 'if you ever aim to be made an instrument of God's glory in saving souls, then at the outset set before your eyes not the honour but the danger of your calling, and humble yourself under the mighty hand of God that he may exalt you in due time' (1 Peter 5:6).

The importance of calling is related to two principal issues, that of perseverance and that of steadfastness in holy living. Isaiah,

Jeremiah and Ezekiel were called in a way which impressed indelibly upon them the awesome holiness of God as well as the high nature of their calling. In face of rebellion and constant resistance by the people and paucity of results these prophets required remarkable perseverance. The glory of God kept them on course. Pastors often have to persevere through lean times when dogged perseverance is required. An absolute assurance of his calling to the ministry will keep a pastor firmly on course. Furthermore a pastor who is always mindful of the glory and holiness of God and is diligent in his disciplines will never fall (2 Peter 1:5-10).

In his exposition of Isaiah's calling Perkins probes deep into the realm of spiritual experience. 'When by the sight and sense of our sins and our misery because of sin, God has driven us out of ourselves so that we find nothing in ourselves but reasons for fear and horror; then he pours the oil of grace and of sweet comfort into our hearts, and refreshes our weary souls with the dew of his mercy.' He suggests that, 'If we look into the Scriptures we shall find God never called people into the state of grace or to any notable work or function in his church without first humbling them.' Further he asks the question, 'Does God bring some great affliction on you? It may be he has some mighty work of grace to do in you, or some great work of mercy to be wrought by you in his church, and is preparing you for it. Learn to say with the holy prophet, "I was mute, I did not open my mouth because it was you who did it (Ps. 39:9)."' Although he does not refer to Jeremiah it is that prophet who records his extreme anguish even to saying he would prefer to be dead than alive (Jer. 15:10) and at one point suggesting that he would not speak any more in God's name (Jer. 20:9).

A call to the ministry must be endorsed by the church: 'If the church of God does not recognise your sufficiency, God is not sending you.'

Perkins gives a warning against academic pride: 'We have many occasions to be puffed up in self-conceit. We see ourselves grow in age, in degrees, in learning, in honour, in reputation and estimation. To many of us God gives an abundant supply of his gifts. But there are many temptations to allure us to pride and over-inflated opinions of our own value. So let us remember that the goal we aim at is not human or carnal. Since our purpose is to save souls, the weapons of our war must not be carnal ones (2 Cor. 10:4) — such as pride, vanity and conceit.'

Application in preaching

Perkins' emphasis on application in preaching is vital. He proceeds along the lines that the pastor should be sensitive to the spiritual state of all the individual members of the congregation. He explores the effect of the application of the Word to all the individual needs. In the chapter on Christ as chief shepherd of the sheep who will not allow the bruised reed to be broken, I described a variety of special needs such as orphans, widows and those struggling with appalling affliction or travelling through desperately difficult times. However, while Christ is compassionate to human suffering of all kinds as illustrated by his healing ten lepers with only one returning to give thanks, suffering does not mean spiritual progress. Suffering may open individuals to spiritual issues but suffering never guarantees spiritual awakening or spiritual hunger. Perkins suggests that the pastor/preacher must think and pray his way through the spiritual conditions of his people.

It has nearly always been the case that congregations consist of both believers and unbelievers. In former generations in countries nominally Christian like England the proportion of unbelievers would be quite high. Perkins stated that that was the case in the congregations of his time.

In preparation to preach he evidently thought through and prayed through the issues of application very carefully. There is the danger particularly with pastors who are diligent in exposition to spend nearly all their time in preparing well-ordered teaching materials and neglect close equally diligent application to the wide variety of individuals before them.

In addressing the subject Perkins defines application as 'the skill by which the doctrine which has been properly drawn from Scripture is handled in ways which are appropriate to the circumstances of the place and time and to the people in the congregation. This is the biblical approach to exposition: "I will feed my flock, and I will make them lie down," says the Lord God. "I will seek what was lost and will bring back what was driven away, bind up the broken and strengthen what was sick" (Ezek. 34:15-16). "And on some have compassion, making a distinction, but others save with fear, pulling them out of the fire" (Jude 22-23).'

Perkins insists that 'the basic principle in application is to know whether the passage is a statement of the law or of the gospel. For when the Word is preached the law and the gospel operate differently. The law exposes the disease of sin and as a side-effect stimulates and stirs it up. But it provides no remedy for it. However, the gospel not only teaches us what is to be done, it also has the power of the Holy Spirit joined to it. When we are regenerated by him we receive the strength we need both to believe the gospel and to do what it commands. The law is, therefore, first in the order of teaching; then comes the gospel.'

In this emphasis Perkins is typical of the Puritan preachers. In the cameo of his life there was that comment about Perkins' preaching, 'The sermons seemed to be "all law and all gospel, all cordials and all corrosives, as the different necessities of people apprehended" them.' If there is no sense of need and no conviction of sin there will never be any progress. Christ came not to call the righteous but sinners to repentance. What is sin? Sin is the transgression of the law. Jesus promised that the Holy Spirit would convince the world of sin, righteousness and judgement. The gospel is irrelevant if these subjects are not preached. I must feel my need of Christ otherwise I will not seek him.

Perkins writes:

> A statement of the law indicates the need for perfect inherent righteousness, of eternal life given through the works of the law, of the sins which are contrary to the law and the curse that is due them. 'For as many as are of the works of the law are under the curse; for it is written, "Cursed is everyone who does not continue in all things which are written in the book of the law, to do them." But that no one is justified by the law in the sight of God is evident, for the just shall live by faith' (Gal. 3:10). 'Brood of vipers! Who warned you to flee from the wrath to come … And even now the axe is laid at the root of the trees. Therefore every tree that does not bear good fruit is cut down and thrown into the fire' (Matt. 3:7,10). By contrast, a statement of the gospel speaks of Christ and his benefits, and of faith being fruitful in good works. For example, 'For God so loved the world that he gave his only begotten Son, that whoever believes in him should not perish but have everlasting life' (John 3:16).

For Perkins, application consisted not only of an astute awareness of law and gospel, the law to convict and the gospel to heal, but preparation in preaching was to think about and pray about and prepare to preach to a variety of people with differing needs.

William Perkins

Categories of hearers

It is very much part of preaching that the preacher thinks carefully about the different kinds of hearers in his congregation. Perkins outlined the different kinds of hearers as follows:

1. Those who are unbelievers and are both ignorant and unteachable

These must first of all be prepared to receive the doctrine of the Word. Jehoshaphat sent Levites throughout the cities of Judah to teach the people, and to draw them away from idolatry (2 Chron. 17:9). This preparation should be partly by discussing or reasoning with them, in order to become aware of their attitude and disposition, and partly by reproving any obvious sin, so that their consciences may be aroused and touched with fear and they may become teachable (see Acts 9:3-5; 16:27-31; 17:17; 17:22-24).

When there is some hope that they have become teachable and prepared, the message of God's Word is to be given to them, usually in basic terms concentrating on general points (as, for example, Paul at Athens, Acts 17:30-31). If there is no positive response to such teaching, then it should be explained in a more detailed way. But if they remain unteachable and there is no real hope of winning them, they should simply be left (Prov. 9:8; Matt. 7:6; Acts 19:9).

2. Those who are teachable, but ignorant

We should instruct such people by means of a catechism (*cf.* Luke 1:4; Acts 18:25-26). A catechism is a brief explanation of the foundational teaching of the Christian faith given in the form of questions and answers. This helps both the understanding and the memory. The content of a catechism, therefore, should be the fundamentals of the Christian faith, a summary of its basic principles (Heb. 5:12).

He continues:

> *Here it is important to recognize the difference between 'milk' and 'strong meat'. These categories refer to the same truth; the difference between them lies in the manner and style of the teaching. 'Milk' is a brief, plain and general explanation of the principles of the faith: that we must believe in one God, and in three persons, Father, Son and Holy Spirit; that we must rely only upon the grace of God in Christ; that we ought to believe in the forgiveness of sins; and when we are taught that we ought to repent, to abstain from evil and to do good.*
>
> *'Strong meat', on the other hand, is a detailed, full, illuminating and clear handling of the doctrine of faith. It includes biblical teaching on such themes as man before the fall, the fall, original and actual sin, human guilt, free will; the mysteries of the Trinity, the two natures of Christ, their union in one person, the office of Christ as Mediator, the imputation of righteousness; faith, grace, and the use of the law. 'Milk' must be set before babes, that is those who are immature or weak in knowledge; strong meat should be given to those who are more mature, that is, to those who are better instructed (1 Cor. 3:1,2; Heb. 5:13).*

3. *There are those who have knowledge, but have never been humbled*

Here we need to see the foundation of repentance stirred up in what Paul calls godly sorrow (1 Cor. 7:8-10). Godly sorrow is grief for sin simply because it is sin. To stir up this affection, the ministry of the law is necessary. This may give birth to a real sense of contrition in the heart, or to terror in the conscience. Although this is not wholesome and profitable on its own, it provides a necessary remedy for subduing sinful stubbornness, and for preparing the mind to become teachable.

In order to arouse this legal sorrow it is appropriate to use some choice section of the law, which may reprove any obvious sin in those who have not yet been humbled. Sorrow for and repentance for even one sin is in substance sorrow for and repentance of all sin (Ps. 32:5; Acts 2:23; 8:22).

Further, if someone who is afflicted with the cross and with outward tragedies has only a worldly sorrow — that is, if he does not mourn for sin *as sin*, but only for the punishment of sin — he is not to be given immediate comfort. Such sorrow must first be transformed into godly sorrow.

Then let the gospel be preached in such a way that the Holy Spirit effectually works salvation. For in renewing men so that they may begin to will and to do what is pleasing to God, the Spirit really and truly produces in them godly sorrow and repentance to salvation.

To the hard-hearted the law must be stressed, and its curse stated clearly along with its threats. The difficulty of obtaining deliverance until people are pricked in their heart should also be taught (Matt. 3:7; 19:16-17; 23:13,33). But when the beginning of genuine sorrow appears they are to be comforted with the gospel.

4. Those who have already been humbled

Here we must carefully consider whether the humbling that has already taken place is complete and sound or only just begun and still light and superficial. It is important that people do not receive comfort sooner than is appropriate. If they do, they may later become hardened in the same way iron which has been cast into the furnace becomes exceptionally hard when it is cold.

Here are some guidelines for dealing with those who are partially humbled. Expound the law to them carefully tempered with the gospel, so that being terrified by their sins and the judgement of God they may at the same time find comfort in the gospel (Gen. 3:9-15; 2 Sam. 12; Acts 8:20-23). Nathan gives us an example here. Through use of a parable he recalled David to an awareness of his sinful condition. When his repentance was certain he pronounced him pardoned.

In this way we see that faith and repentance and the comforts of the gospel ought to be taught and offered to those who have been fully humbled (Matt. 9:13; Luke 4:18; Acts 2:37-38).

5. *Those who already believe. We must teach them*:

   a. The gospel: the biblical teaching on justification, sanctification and perseverance.
   b. The law: but as it applies to those who are no longer under its curse, so that they may be taught how to bear the fruit of a new obedience in keeping with their repentance (Rom. 8:1; 1 Tim. 1:9). Here Paul's teaching in Romans serves as a model.
   c. Although someone who is righteous and holy in the sight of God should not be threatened, the curse of the law to their remaining sin should still be stressed. As a father may show his sons what he will do as punishment to induce a proper sense of fear of doing wrong, so meditation on the curse of the law should be frequently encouraged in true believers, to discourage abusing the mercy of God by sinful living, and to increase humility. Our sanctification is partial as yet. In order that the remnants of sin may be destroyed we must

always begin with meditation on the law, and with a sense of our sin, in order to be brought to rest in the gospel.

6. *Those who have fallen back*

Some may have partly departed from the state of grace, either in faith or in lifestyle. This is important and relevant because we all know of those who did run well but now have fallen back and some so badly that we wonder if they were truly saved in the first place.

Failure in faith is either in the knowledge of the doctrine of the gospel or in apprehending Christ. Failure in knowledge involves declining into error, whether in a secondary or fundamental doctrine. In this situation the specific doctrine which counteracts their error should be expounded and taught. We need to stress its importance to them, along with the doctrine of repentance. But we must do this with a brotherly affection, as Paul says in Galatians 6:1 (*cf.* 2 Tim. 2:25).

A fall from apprehending Christ leads to despair. In order to restore such we need to diagnose their condition and then prescribe the remedy. We must analyse either the cause of their temptation or their condition. The diagnosis of the cause can be done appropriately by confession (*cf.* James 5:17). But to prevent such confession being turned into an instrument of torture it must be governed by these principles:

a. It ought to be done freely and not under any compulsion. Salvation does not depend on it.
b. It must not be a confession of all sins, but only of those which eat at the conscience and may lead to even greater spiritual danger if they are not dealt with.
c. Such confession should chiefly be made to pastors, but with the

understanding that it may be confidentially shared with other reliable men in the church.

The diagnosis of a person's spiritual status involves investigating whether they are under the law or under grace. In order to clarify this we must probe and question to discover from them whether they are displeased with themselves, because they have displeased God. Do they hate *sin as sin*? This is the foundation of the repentance which brings salvation. Then, secondly, we must ask whether they have or feel in their heart a desire to be reconciled with God. This is the groundwork for a living faith.

When the diagnosis is complete, the remedy must be prescribed and applied from the gospel. It is twofold.

a. That their sin is pardonable.
b. That the promises of grace are made generally to all who believe.
c. They are not made to specific individuals; they therefore exclude no one.
d. That the will to believe is itself faith (Ps. 145:19; Rev. 21:6).
e. That sin does not abolish grace but rather (since God turns everything to the good of those who are his) can lead to further illustrations of it.
f. That in this fallen and sinful world all of God's works are done by means which are contrary to him!

I have quoted Perkins at length to illustrate the thoroughness of his practice with regard to application.

The Art of Prophesying ends on positive notes of encouragement. This is important as there followed a time of severe persecution. Soon after Perkins' death a number resolved to sail for New England in quest of freedom from persecution. After the Great Ejection of 1662 came a time of severe suffering for about 2000, mostly Puritan ministers, ejected from the Established Church. Much comfort would be administered to these pastors through Perkins' book especially in such words as these: 'If he sends them he will defend and protect them, so that not even one of their hairs is able to perish. If he sends them he will provide for them and reward them adequately. He will honour them in the hearts of his own people and magnify them in the face of their enemies. And lastly, if he sends them he will pay their wages: an eternal weight of comfort here and of glory in heaven.' He concludes with the text from Daniel 12:3:

Those who are wise shall shine,
Like the brightness of the firmament,
And those who turn many to righteousness
Like the stars for ever and ever.

THE REVEREND and LEARNED,
Mr. RICHARD BAXTER.

Done from an Original painting in the Possession of the Rev. Mr. Benjamin Fawcett, at Kidderminster.
Published by J. Spilsbury Engraver, Map & Printseller, in Russel Court Covent Garden, Aug.t 1. 1763.

Richard Baxter

6

Richard Baxter

The pastor as evangelist

Our role model will be the English Puritan Richard Baxter (1615–1691). I will proceed as follows:

An outline of Baxter's life
Baxter as a pastor and evangelist
Baxter's book — *A Call to the Unconverted*
Baxter's book — *The Reformed Pastor.*

An outline of Baxter's life

Richard Baxter was born in 1615. Unlike almost all the better-known English Puritan ministers he did not enjoy an education at Oxford or Cambridge Universities. He attended the modest Donnington Free School, and thereafter he was self-taught. An avid reader, he studied widely in a variety of subjects. In this way he became a man of exceptional knowledge and debating ability. He was ordained deacon by the Bishop of Worcester in 1638. For a brief time, 1641–1642, he worked as lecturer and curate at

Kidderminster. In 1642 the country was embroiled in civil war. Richard served as a chaplain in the Parliamentary army until 1647 and then returned to Kidderminster as vicar, where he served until 1661. These fourteen years, aged thirty-two to forty-six, were remarkable because of the spiritual transformation wrought in the town. So blessed was the town that Kidderminster became a landmark in English evangelical history. I will describe that work in detail presently.

Toward the end of his time in Kidderminster a widow by the name of Mary Hanmer came to stay in the town in order to benefit from Baxter's ministry. She was accompanied by her sixteen-year-old daughter Margaret who was worldly and indifferent to the gospel. Over the next four years Margaret was affected by the ministry and at the age of twenty was converted. She had in the process fallen in love with Richard who regarded celibacy as ideal for a minister. This he proclaimed with enthusiasm, a view in strong contrast with that of the English Puritans who emphasized the biblical doctrine of marriage and the family. When Richard left Kidderminster to live in London in 1660 he used what influence he could to gain a fair deal for the Puritans. Mary and her daughter Margaret followed him and lived nearby.

The Act of Uniformity passed by Parliament in 1662 was rigid and violently against the consciences of the Puritans. It drove them out of the Church of England. About 2,000 Puritan ministers suffered the loss of their livings in what is historically called the Great Ejection. This of course included Baxter. Richard's life was devastated. Now his *raison d'être*, the main purpose of his life, was cruelly stripped away. He was a natural pastor — without a parish; a born preacher — without a pulpit! His justification for celibacy was gone! He married Margaret on 19 September 1662. Now Margaret was always there for him, comforting him, caring for him in his frequent illnesses, shouldering all the practical concerns of his life.

Living with Margaret was the chief consolation enjoyed by Baxter during the following grim years.[1] The rest of Baxter's life was one of harassment. He was imprisoned for about a week in Clerkenwell in 1669 and for twenty-one months at Southwark 1685–1686. He never enjoyed robust health and had to contend with serious bouts of illness.

In November 1672 Baxter preached openly for the first time in ten years. Margaret (1636–1681) generously put her considerable inheritance to use to ensure that Richard exercised an effective public ministry. She hired a public hall which could seat 800 in one of the most needy parts of London and employed a staff to assist Richard in his ministry.

During the times of exclusion from public ministry Richard used his time to write. His writings were as numerous as those of John Owen. Unlike Owen, who is probably the most profound and most reliable theologian in the English language, Baxter was Neonomian and Amyraldian.[2] Sadly this caused theological confusion in the next generation or two.[3] Readers of his three classic works *The Saints' Everlasting Rest*, being an exposition of heaven, *A Call to the Unconverted* and *The Reformed Pastor* will not spot these errors. Baxter is easier to read than Owen. His most extensive writing is called *A Christian Directory* which covers every aspect of Christian living from a practical point of view. It is in practical application of the Scriptures that we see Baxter at his best. He possessed a tremendous gift for constraining and compelling the conscience to obedience.

Richard was always zealous about missionary work. He was a prime mover in the establishment of the Society for the Propagation of the Gospel in New England. John Eliot, famous as 'the apostle to the American Indians', found in Baxter a sterling supporter. In his last illness in 1691 Baxter read the *Life of Eliot* and wrote to

Increase Mather the author, 'I thought I had been near dying at twelve o'clock in bed; but your book revived me. I knew much of Mr Eliot's opinions, by many letters which I received from him. There was no man on earth I honoured above him. It is his evangelical work that is the apostolic succession for which I plead.'

Baxter as pastor and evangelist

As an evangelist/pastor Baxter was supreme. The success of the gospel in Kidderminster under his leadership was unique. It is hard to find anything in English evangelical history to compare with it.

The town consisted of about 800 homes and a population of between 2000 and 4000 people. Baxter found that they were 'an ignorant, rude and revelling people'. An amazing change took place. 'When I first entered on my labours I took special notice of every one that was humbled, reformed or converted; but when I had laboured long, it pleased God that the converts were so many, that I could not afford time for such particular observations … families and considerable numbers at once … came in and grew up I scarce knew how.' Baxter's method was to visit house by house and to be very direct in the matter of knowing God with saving faith.

The church building could accommodate a thousand. Five galleries were added to accommodate the increasing congregations.

When Baxter came to this poor town where weaving was the principal industry, it was a spiritual wilderness. When he left, it was a beautiful, well-tended garden. 'On the Lord's days, you might hear an hundred families singing psalms and repeating sermons as you passed through the streets. When I first came there, only about one family in a street worshipped God and called on his name, and when I left there were some streets where there was not a family which did not do so, in that they professed serious godliness which gave us hope of their sincerity.'

Later Baxter could write: 'though I have now been absent from them for about six years, and they have been assaulted with pulpit-calumnies and slanders, with threatenings — yet they stand fast and keep their integrity. Many of them have gone to God, some are removed and some in prison, but not one that I hear of have fallen off, nor forsaken their uprightness.' When, in December 1743, George Whitefield visited Kidderminster he wrote to a friend: 'I was greatly refreshed to find what a sweet savour of good Mr Baxter's doctrine, works and discipline remained to this day.'

The main difference between Baxter and most other pastors, then and now, is that he combined personal direct witness, one on one, with preaching. Too often pastors are content to confine their gospel witness to the pulpit.

The great commission of Matthew 28:16-20 falls into two parts. First, we are to make disciples of all nations. Second, we are to teach the disciples the whole counsel of the Bible. Too often when evangelism has taken place successfully a church becomes institutional and is concerned only with its own internal welfare. The vision to reach the lost is forgotten. Evangelism is neglected. Reaching out to all the lost souls of the world must ever remain the top priority of the Christian Church. In this the pastor should lead from the front to initiate evangelistic effort and to seek in every way possible to encourage the members to use their gifts. If a pastor is unable himself to lead, he should appoint those who are able, to fulfil this ever-present responsibility. Many avenues of evangelism are open in western society where we are not forbidden to promulgate the gospel. Often there are openings to teach in schools. House to house evangelism is possible. Open-air evangelism, if well planned, can be successful. It is not enough to expect non-Christian people to come to church. We have to reach out to them and visit them where they are.

The burden to reach so many lost people is always on a true pastor's heart. He can never escape this pressing reality day or night. His only hope of success is to mobilize his people and teach them by example and initiative to evangelize. Baxter's exhortations ring with sincerity because he practised what he preached. Like a military officer he led his soldiers into battle. He did not give commands from a safety zone.

It can be a temptation to resort to literature evangelism and think that if we distribute booklets or tracts to every house then the work is done. Certainly that is better than nothing, but talking to people face to face is the best way.

Baxter made it his business to visit every house in Kidderminster. His enterprise was richly rewarded as we have seen. His method was catechism, that is, question and answer. That method will not be effective today as we will soon be rejected if we think that we can be so direct with the non-churchgoers. An effective method of evangelism today is the use of courses which come in a package such as *Christianity Explored*. These courses of instruction as to what Christianity is all about are structured for use in house groups. Details of this fine work can be found on the *Christianity Explored* web site.

Baxter's book — *A Call to the Unconverted*

The manner in which Baxter addressed people in public or in private is reflected in his book *A Call to the Unconverted*, 20,000 copies of which were sold in the first year and which was translated into a number of languages. The text opened up is Ezekiel 33:11: 'As surely as I live, declares the Sovereign LORD, I take no pleasure in the death of the wicked, but rather that they turn from their ways and live. Turn! Turn from your evil ways! Why will you die, O house of Israel?'

This book throbs with passion and desire for the wicked to turn from their sinful lives. The message of this classic work is set out under seven headings:

1. It is the unchangeable law of God that wicked men must turn or die.
2. It is the promise of God that the wicked shall live, if they turn.
3. God takes pleasure in men's conversion and salvation, but not in their death or damnation; he had rather they would return and live, than go on and die.
4. This is a most certain truth, which because God would not have men to question, he has confirmed it solemnly by his oath.
5. The Lord redoubles his commands and persuasions to the wicked to turn.
6. The Lord condescends to reason the case with them and asks the wicked why they will die.
7. If, after all this, the wicked will not return, it is not God's desire that they should perish, but their own wilfulness being the cause of their damnation, they die because they will die.

Baxter not only warns of the eternal death that awaits the unrepentant but he seeks to persuade sinners to turn to Christ because of the wonders and blessings of salvation. The following is typical of how he sets out the wonders of God's grace:

You shall be made living members of Christ and be renewed after the image of God, being quickened with a new and heavenly life and saved from the tyranny of Satan and the dominion of sin. You will be justified from the curse of the law, having pardon of all the sins of the whole of your life, being accepted by God and made his sons. You have liberty to boldly call him Father, and go to him by prayer in all your needs with a promise of acceptance. You will have the Holy Spirit to dwell with you, to sanctify and guide you. You will have part in the brotherhood and prayers of the saints. You will be fitted for God's service, freed from the dominion of sin, be useful and a blessing where you live and have the promise of this life and that which is to come. You will have no need of anything which is for your good and you will be enabled to bear necessary afflictions. You will know God's presence especially in the ordinances, and be heirs of heaven while you live on earth. Your status on earth may be low but your peace and happiness will be incomparably greater than your misery.

Baxter's book has been transposed into modern English by John Blanchard and republished with the title *An Invitation to Live*. Published by EP Books, this excellent work is out of print at present, but hopefully if demand returns it will become available again.

Baxter as a pastor as reflected in his book *The Reformed Pastor*

We come now to consider the work of the pastor as he has to care for his flock. In this we observe Baxter's attitude and practice, which is clearly described in his book *The Reformed Pastor*.

The members of the 'Worcester Association', the ministers fraternal of which Baxter was the moving spirit, had committed themselves to adopt the policy of systematic parochial catechizing on Baxter's plan. They fixed a day of fasting and prayer, to seek God's blessing on the undertaking, and asked Baxter to preach. When the day came, however, Baxter was too ill to go; so he published the material he had prepared, a thorough exposition and application of Acts 20:28. It bore the title *The Reformed Pastor* and was published in 1656. It turned out to be a famous book which has been used in every generation up to the present time. For instance, the Banner of Truth edition, with a superb introduction by J. I. Packer, appeared in 1974 and editions have followed in 1979, 1983, 1989, 1994, 1997, 1999 and 2001.

By the word 'Reformed' in the title Baxter did not mean Calvinistic in doctrine but renewed in practice. This treatise is spiritual dynamite and was recognized as such from its inception. In the month after its publication a correspondent wrote: 'O man greatly beloved! The Lord has revealed his secret things to you, for which many thousand souls in England shall rise up and bless God for you.'

This has proved to be correct. Baxter's *The Reformed Pastor* is still the best manual for the pastor's duty in the English language. Nothing has exceeded its power and effectiveness. It is a must for every pastor.

J. I. Packer in the Banner of Truth edition suggests that its energy and evocative power leap across three centuries. He describes three outstanding qualities.

The first is *its energy*. 'Its words have hands and feet.' Baxter had piercing eyes and he certainly had piercing words. 'His book blazes with white hot zeal, evangelistic fervour, and eagerness to convince.'

The second quality is that *the book has reality*. 'It is honest and straight. It is often said, quite fairly, that any Christian who seriously thinks that without Christ men are lost, and who seriously loves his neighbour, will not be able to rest for the thought that all around him people are going to hell, but will lay himself out unstintingly to convert others as his prime task in life; and any Christian who fails so to live undermines the credibility of his faith, for if he himself cannot take it seriously as a guide for living, why should anyone else? Nowhere is this consistency more forcefully exposed than in *The Reformed Pastor*: for here we meet a passionate love and a terribly honest, earnest, straightforward Christian, thinking and talking about the lost with perfect realism, insisting that we must be content to accept any degree of discomfort, poverty, overwork and loss of material good, if only souls might be saved, and setting us a marvellously vivid example in his own person of what this may involve.'

Third, the book is *a model of rationality*. By this I take Packer to mean that it makes sense. Responsibility is spelled out clearly. 'Grace enters by the understanding.' Baxter insisted that ministers must preach about eternal issues as men who feel what they say, and are earnest about matters of eternal life and death. He also insisted that church discipline be practised to show that God will not accept sin.

In his exposition of Acts 20:28 Baxter expounds the exhortation, 'Keep watch over yourselves.' He then opens up the meaning of what it is to watch all the sheep of the flock. He begins with the unconverted and includes them in his sights. He then exhorts to careful oversight of families and insists that we must be faithful in admonishing offenders. As to the manner in which oversight is to be maintained this must be purely for God and the salvation of souls. It must be performed diligently and thoroughly and prudently and orderly. The work must be done with plainness and simplicity, with humility, with a mixture of severity and mildness, with seriousness, earnestness and zeal, with tender love to our people, with patience, reverence, and spirituality, with earnest desires for success and with a deep sense of our own insufficiency.

Richard Baxter

The book is brimming with wisdom. For instance I quote this section on pastoral work:

> *The ministerial work must be carried on prudently and orderly. Milk must go before strong meat; the foundation must be laid before we attempt to raise the superstructure. Children must not be dealt with as men of full stature. Men must be brought into a state of grace, before we can expect from them the works of grace. The work of conversion and repentance from dead works, and faith in Christ, must be first and frequently and thoroughly taught. We must not ordinarily go beyond the capacities of our people, nor teach them perfection, that have not learned the first principles of religion: for, as Gregory of Nyssa said: 'We teach not infants the deep precepts of science, but the first letters and then syllables... So the guides of the Church do first propound to their hearers certain documents which are as the elements; and so by degrees open to them the more perfect and mysterious matters.'*

Baxter goes on to observe that the church exercised a ministry of disciplined instruction with their catechumens before they baptized them, and would not lay unpolished stones into the building.

With help from Baxter we have seen something of the extent of a pastor's demanding responsibilities. A strong spiritual life is necessary to carry the burdens and fulfil the demands of preaching and pastoring.

PAINTED BY C.W.PEALE.   ENGD BY J.SARTAIN.

Jonathan Edwards,

7

Jonathan Edwards

The pastor as a theologian

Every pastor is required to be a reliable theologian. His studies in theology will be foundational to his entire ministry.

Jonathan Edwards is an example of a pastor who majored in theology. His writing has provided a rich resource of materials for the wider Church ever since. The 300th anniversary of his birth was celebrated in 2003. During that year a variety of meetings took place to commemorate that event. For instance 2,500 gathered for a conference in Minneapolis at the church led by Dr John Piper.

Firstly, for those who may know little about him, I offer a sketch of Edwards' life. Secondly, I will outline the most significant aspects of Edwards' writing ministry which has had an ongoing impact on the Church. I will do this through a review of some of his most influential books. Thirdly, I will seek to challenge readers with a consideration of Edwards as a theologian. This was evident in his love for theology and in his disciplined methods of meditation and study.

A biographical sketch

Jonathan Edwards (1703–1758) is America's best-known theologian and philosopher. He is remembered for America's most famous sermon which was on Deuteronomy 32:35: 'Their foot shall slide in due time.' This is a terrifying sermon about hell. He titled it 'Sinners in the hands of an angry God'.

Jonathan was raised in a Christian family and had four older sisters and six younger. All of them grew to six foot tall! Of Timothy Edwards it was said in the village of East Windsor that he had sixty feet of daughters!

Jonathan was converted at the age of seventeen. He studied for BA and then MA at Yale College. This was followed by a short pastorate in 1723 in Bolton, Connecticut. From 1724–26 he worked as a tutor at Yale.

In 1726 Jonathan was called to be assistant pastor in Northampton to his grandfather on his mother's side, the well-known Solomon Stoddard. In 1727 he married Sarah Pierrepont. She was seventeen. Over the next twenty-three years she bore three sons and eight daughters.

Solomon Stoddard was minister at Northampton for over sixty years. He died in 1729. Edwards, then aged twenty-six, became the sole minister. The country was young and the population small. Northampton consisted of about 200 houses and about 1000 people, and the Congregational church was the only church in the town. Edwards found that the congregation was mostly unconverted and bored by preaching. But in 1735 a remarkable spiritual awakening took place along the Connecticut valley and in Northampton in particular. Within one year in Northampton about 300 appeared to be soundly converted.

Two years later Edwards' description of this remarkable revival was published with the title *A Narrative of Surprising Conversions*. This aroused widespread interest in revival on both sides of the Atlantic.

The 1735 revival at Northampton was a foretaste of a major spiritual awakening which spread all over New England. This had its beginnings in 1739 but grew in power and expanded geographically reaching times of extraordinary power in August and September 1741.

Fanaticism and wild behaviour in this revival led to criticism and opposition. Those against the revival were called 'Old Lights'. Those in favour (and they formed the majority) were called 'New Lights'. Edwards used his pen to describe and defend the awakening.

A New England minister wrote: 'Immediately preceded by a long season of coldness and indifference, the Great Awakening broke upon the slumbering churches like a thunderbolt rushing out of a clear sky.' There were signs of preparation. Preachers had been prepared. A spirit of prayer was found in some of the churches.

The catalyst in this revival was George Whitefield who reached Philadelphia in November 1739. He was twenty-five years old. He spent time with Gilbert Tennent, one of the leading preachers of that time. Tennent shared with Whitefield descriptions of remarkable outpourings of the Holy Spirit that he had witnessed. In the months that followed revival spread. Pastors reported: 'God is present in our assemblies.'

Large crowds flocked to hear Whitefield. A farmer, Nathan Cole, wrote a description of his experience in his horseback journey with his wife. From his farm to a place called Middletown was twelve miles. At about 8.00am Cole received the message that Whitefield was due to preach at Middletown at 10.00am that morning. Cole left his work immediately and called to his wife to get ready. He and his wife took turns to ride the horse with Nathan running when it was his turn. As they drew nearer, he saw a cloud or fog rising which turned out to be a cloud of dust rising from horse galloping. A great stream of riders was on its way to hear the preacher. In his journey of twelve miles Cole saw not one man at work in his field. All had left with the same purpose. As he drew near to the place appointed he could see ferry boats bringing loads of people across the great river. It was reported that between 3,000 and 4,000 gathered. Nathan Cole testified that, 'this young slim youth looked almost angelical — clothed with authority from the great God and a sweet solemnity sat upon his brow — and my hearing him preach gave me a heart wound and by God's blessing my old foundations were broken up and I saw my righteousness would not save me.'

At this time Whitefield spent twenty days preaching daily in the Boston area. According to a newspaper report, at his farewell service 23,000 gathered to hear him preach. The fruitfulness which followed Whitefield's ministry at this time proved it to be a time of great increase in the churches.

It was when he left Boston that he stayed with Jonathan Edwards at Northampton.

Edwards wrote: 'Whitefield preached four sermons in the meeting house (besides a private lecture at my house). The congregation was extraordinarily melted by each sermon, almost the whole assembly being in tears for a great part of the time.' Ninety-five new members were welcomed into the church in the months that followed.

Mrs Sarah Edwards wrote to her brother James: 'Whitefield is truly a remarkable man, and during his visit, has I think verified all we have heard of him. He makes less of the doctrines than our American preachers generally do and aims more at affecting the heart. He is a born orator. You have already heard of his deep-toned yet clear and melodious voice. It is perfect music.'

'It is wonderful to see what a spell he casts over an audience by proclaiming the simplest truths of the Bible. I have seen upwards of a thousand people hang on his words with breathless silence, broken only by an occasional half-suppressed sob.'

Edwards and Whitefield became loyal friends. A point of disagreement however was over Whitefield's 'inclination to impulses'.

It was in 1741 that the revival spread more powerfully all over New England. This was a spiritual awakening more general and extraordinary in its power than anything ever known before. In some areas concern about eternity came gradually but in others dramatically. For instance on 23 November at Middleborough seventy-six were struck to enquire what they could do to be saved.

About fifteen ministers devoted themselves to itinerant evangelism. Edwards also devoted time to an itinerant ministry in order to reap the harvest. It was at Enfield at this time that he preached his most famous sermon, 'Sinners in the hands of an Angry God'. So great were the outcries of anguish under that sermon that he was not able to complete it.

The months of August and September were the most remarkable in 1741. Meetings were characterized by intense spiritual experiences. This was the case especially in smaller gatherings in homes. Frequently there were outcries, faintings and convulsions. These concerned conviction of sin and distress. There were in those liberated vibrant expressions of joy unspeakable and full of glory. Sometimes individuals were so overcome that they were not able to return home but were obliged to stay all night at the house where they had met.

Those opposed to the revival criticized the meetings as extravagant. One preacher, Davenant by name, was eccentric. He encouraged excess. By his bad example he brought disrepute to the revival but later repented.

It was at this time that Edwards was led to write his principal books on revival which have earned him the title 'The Theologian of Revival'. He defended the New England revival as a genuine and wonderful work of God.

It was on Thursday 28 May 1747, at the time when Edwards was preparing for publication the treatise calling for a Concert of Prayer, that David Brainerd rode into the parsonage yard at Northampton. Edwards, whose mind was engaged in the vision of worldwide mission, had only met Brainerd once before. Brainerd shared with Edwards his experiences with the Indians. He described the remarkable work of the Holy Spirit that he had seen among them. Brainerd, aged only twenty-nine, died that same year from tuberculosis in the Edwards' home. Jonathan Edwards used Brainerd's diaries to write his biography which was the first modern missionary biography. For over a century it was the most popular book on missions. Many were called to the mission field through reading the biography of David Brainerd.

During the 1740s Edwards sought to reform his church with regard to the Lord's Table. It was the custom established by his famous predecessor, Solomon Stoddard, that those who made no profession of conversion could partake of the Lord's Table. Edwards' efforts to reform this unbiblical practice led to increasing opposition and eventually to his dismissal from the church in

Northampton in 1750. Only the men voted. Edwards was rejected by 230 votes to 23.

Here we have the best-known minister in New England humiliated by dismissal from his church. 'The scene of America's greatest theologian and colonial America's most powerful thinker being run out of town and forced into exile in a frontier village has intrigued observers ever since.'[1] Destitution loomed for the Edwards' large family. However, after about a year a call came to lead a tiny church in the dangerous frontier village of Stockbridge. There were only twelve families in membership and to this was added the work of pastoring about 250 Mohican and 60 Mohawk Indians. The large Edwards family moved to Stockbridge in 1751. Jonathan now devoted more time to writing. Two of his important books, *The Freedom of the Will* and *Original Sin,* were written at this time.

In 1757 Aaron Burr, the president of Princeton College, died and Edwards reluctantly responded to the call to take that position. It was not to be. He died suddenly in 1758 from a smallpox inoculation.

The impact of Jonathan Edwards on church history

Edwards was lightly esteemed by the generation that followed him. Ezra Stiles, President of Yale, observed in 1771 that he could estimate that only forty-five ministers out of 500 or 600 in New England admired Edwards as an author. Sixteen years later in 1787, Stiles used extremely disparaging terms about Edwards' writings. He said in effect that they would pass into oblivion and be found only in rubbish heaps.[2] It is wonderful to observe that 300 years after his birth, Edwards' books are being published more than ever before.

All Edwards' writings have been gathered, edited and published in twenty-five volumes by Yale University Press. Today Edwards receives more attention than any other American theologian. Dozens of books and hundreds of articles about Edwards have been written.

He was unique in his day inasmuch as he could respond to and interact with the philosophers of his time. That aspect of his ministry is important and is of interest to some. I believe that Edwards' greatest contribution to the Church is in the area of revival.

Six of his books relate to the subject of revival. As noted above, these have earned him the title 'The Theologian of Revival'. In this way Edwards represents a watershed in church history. He marks a new beginning — the age of revivals. Two of these books describe and defend the revivals in New England. One is the biography of David Brainerd in which there is a description of the revival among the Indians.

Having witnessed the power of God in the revivals of 1735 and 1740–41 and later having read David Brainerd's descriptions of the revival among the Indians, Edwards was convinced that outpourings of the Holy Spirit were the way in which the whole world would eventually be turned to Christ. Writing to Whitefield in December 1740, he outlined his view that the proud empire of Satan would fall throughout the earth and the kingdom of Christ be established from one end of the earth to the other.[3]

A humble attempt

The theology of victory, that is, that Christ will eventually triumph over his enemies on earth, led Edwards in 1747 to write an appeal for special prayer to be made for revival. This began with an exposition of Zechariah 8:20-23. This is a small book with a long title, which points to the main parts of the exposition.

An Humble Attempt to Promote Explicit Agreement and Visible Union of God's People in Extraordinary Prayer for the Revival of Religion and the Advancement of Christ's Kingdom on Earth, Pursuant to Scripture Promises and Prophecies concerning the Last Time.

Happily this book was reprinted in 2004 with the shorter title *Praying Together for True Revival.*[4] Edwards contends that the description of many peoples gathering urgently for prayer has yet to be fulfilled. This urgent intercession is motivated by faith in the promises of God's Word which have not yet been fulfilled. Such earnest prayer in itself is prompted and promoted by the Holy Spirit as described by Zechariah: 'And I will pour out on the house of David and the inhabitants of Jerusalem a spirit of grace and supplication. They will look on me, the one they have pierced, and they will mourn for him as one mourns for an only child, and grieve bitterly for him as one grieves for a firstborn son' (Zech. 12:10).

Great theologian that he was, Edwards was astute to observe that the intercession for which he pleaded was not for success for man's satisfaction and praise, but for God's glory. At its very heart was a seeking of the Lord himself: 'You will seek me and find me when you seek me with all your heart: I will be found by you, declares the LORD, and will bring you back from captivity' (Jer. 29:10-14). Edwards observes that Zechariah describes many peoples and strong nations. The world of peoples of the eighteenth century was small in comparison to the twenty-first century. He was not in a position to see Christianity come to life in a huge nation like China as we have done. He did foresee in Zechariah's prophecy a powerful unity of purpose in those gathering to pray which Edwards describes as 'explicit agreement and visible union'. Here are the signs of the complete unity for which our Lord prayed (John 17:21).

Edwards describes the coming powerful advancement of the gospel. Readers today will find this breathtaking and hardly credible in face of the opposition of so many false religions. Readers are unlikely to agree with the way Edwards interprets some of the Scriptures and I would not use the second part of Daniel and the book of Revelation as he does, but the manner in which he applies Daniel 2:35 and 44 is compelling. Edwards anticipates that once the spirit of prayer is given to the Church, God's wider purposes will be swiftly fulfilled. He sees Psalm 102:16-17 as especially relevant: 'For the LORD will rebuild Zion and appear in his glory. He will respond to the prayer of the destitute; he will not despise their plea.'

The LORD is merciful to those who, in desperate need and distress, call on him. Edwards was fully aware of those who would not agree with his views and he answers objections. He expounds the defeat of Antichrist in a way very different from views held by many today.

Edwards' call to prayer was heeded and implemented and lay at the heart of the second great awakening in 1792–1840, sometimes called 'the forgotten revival'. It also lay at the genesis of the great missionary movement of the first part of the nineteenth century.

As early as 1754 John Gillies collected descriptions of revivals and published a series of twenty-one papers.[5] For instance, among many examples he cited, he believed that remarkable revivals in parts of the Netherlands had come in answer to the Concert of Prayer in Britain and America.[6]

Edwards' book on a call to prayer for revival is exceedingly relevant for us today. Much of what he foresaw by way of an irresistible spread of the gospel to all nations is now evident. Prayer for global revival and a mighty surge forward is now more urgent than ever.

There are other books by Edwards which also call for our attention. We will look at three.

The Religious Affections

This book was first published in 1746, with further editions published subsequently. This is the best of all the writings of Edwards. It is profound and edifying in every respect and takes its place in Christian literature as a classic. Edwards begins by defining what he means by affections. He shows that this matter is one of eternal life or death, for if we are not joined to the Triune God in our affections we are lost eternally.

The rest of the 382-page treatise is divided into two parts. First he shows what are no certain signs that religious affections are truly gracious. This is vital as we consider all religious revivals. The very reason for writing this treatise was to show that in a revival there is much excitement but that in itself does not mean anything unless there is an inward spiritual work joining souls to Christ.

That religious affections are very great is not a sign. That there are great bodily effects is no sign. He goes on to show that all kinds of fervour and zeal in themselves do not constitute certainty of a genuine work of the Holy Spirit that will result in eternal life. He shows that moving testimonies and great confidence are no sign. With hindsight, passionate experiences can be recognized as having carnal elements. Satan is always active in revival to spoil things as much as possible. Fanaticism and wild behaviour during the revival of 1740-41 brought disrepute to the gospel and aroused opposition to the revival as a whole. Afterwards there were those who fell away. All this sounds very discouraging to us in our day of little zeal and fervour. But we must remember that the whole purpose of Edwards' writing on this theme was to defend and uphold the reality of revival which is always a mixed work. So what does constitute a true work of God?

The second part of *The Religious Affections* is positive. It is about twice as long as the first section. Here Edwards reveals penetration and depth of thought and, above all, biblical reality that is quite amazing. This is greatly needed in our times of superficial religion.

These are the main headings of this positive exposition by Edwards. Gracious affections are from divine influence. Their object is the excellence of divine things. They are founded on the moral excellency of divine revelation. They arise from divine illumination. They are attended by a conviction of certainty. They are attended with evangelical humiliation. They are attended with a change of nature. They beget and promote the temper of Jesus. Gracious affections soften the heart. They have a beautiful symmetry and proportion. False affections rest satisfied in themselves. Religious affections have their fruit in Christian practice, which is the chief sign to others and to ourselves.

The History of Redemption

In this treatise, ambitious in its scope, Edwards surveys God's purpose in the history of the world. He believed that this purpose was to subdue this sinful earth under the Prince of Peace (Ps. 110:1). Outpourings of the Holy Spirit are the practical means by which this will eventually be achieved.

Worldwide dominion of the gospel suggested by Edwards seems an utter impossibility. He did not foresee this as a sudden miraculous achievement but rather as a conquest of immense difficulty that would take place stage by stage. As mentioned above, if we compare the world of Edwards' day with our own, we observe that evangelical Christianity has spread all over the world. Christianity has taken up residence in more nations now than ever before. As the Bible is translated into many languages we can see that there is no limit to its pervasive influence. Many examples can be cited. In 1900 the presence of the gospel in South Korea was like a mustard seed. A powerful revival was experienced in North Korea in 1907. The effects of this revival have been felt in South Korea while in North Korea Christians have been severely persecuted and driven underground. Today there are about seven million Evangelicals in South Korea out of a population of forty-nine million. South Korea sends out over 21,500 missionaries to about 175 other nations.

Revival is always relevant. We who are Bible-believing Christians confess that we constantly stand in need of revival. Our churches urgently need to be revived in zeal. Revival also raises the subject of true conversion. Many in the Great Awakening who thought they were Christians discovered that they were not. They were spiritually awakened. Revival brings spiritual reality.

Edwards draws our attention to the fact that revivals have a central place in the purposes of God. Universal dominion is promised to Christ but this will never be brought about without powerful interventions by the Holy Spirit. The opposition to spiritual life is great and false religion holds sway. That was the case at the time of Pentecost. The ruling body of the Jews, the Sanhedrin, had succeeded in sending Jesus to crucifixion. The Sanhedrin was bitterly hostile to the apostles but in spite of that opposition the Church was established in Jerusalem. Pentecost was the first revival and a prototype of outpourings of the Holy Spirit to come.

J. I. Packer provides us with helpful insights on revival when he writes:

> What exactly happens in a reviving visitation from God, gradual or sudden, brief or prolonged, large or small-scale, as the case may be? From Scripture, and particularly from the Acts of the Apostles, which is a narrative from the archetypal revival era, we can put together a general answer to that question, all the specifics of which can be illustrated, one way or another, from Edwards' revival writings. To be sure, no two episodes of revival are identical, if only because the various individuals and communities to which, and the various cultural backgrounds against which, the reviving of religion takes place, have their own unique features and in every narrative of revival these should be noted. But the same generic pattern appears everywhere. Revival is God's touching minds and hearts in an arresting, devastating, exalting way, to draw them to himself through working from the inside out, rather than from the outside in. It is God's accelerating, intensifying and extending the work of grace that goes on in every Christian's life, but is sometimes overshadowed and somewhat smothered by the impact of other forces. It is the near presence of God, giving new power to the gospel. It is the Holy Spirit's sensitising of souls to divine realities and so generating deep-level responses to God in the form of faith and repentance, praise and prayer, love and joy, works of benevolence and service and initiatives of outreach and sharing.[7]

Charity and its fruits

This 368-page book was published after Edwards' death. It is based upon a series of sermons on 1 Corinthians 13, preached in 1738.

The practical teaching of this treatise represents the very heart of Edwards' theology and the theme is very close to his exposition *The Religious Affections*. True conversion will result in a behaviour of love which is the opposite of the infighting and quarrelling that was developing in the town of Northampton. The book concludes with an exposition of heaven which is a world of love. Heaven is where the fountain overflows in streams and rivers of love and delight.

The exposition of the opening verses evidences a very clear doctrine of cessationism. 'Love is more excellent than the extraordinary gifts of the Spirit.' Very clearly Edwards explains the difference between the ordinary and the extraordinary gifts and operations of the Spirit. He shows from Matthew 7:22-23 that the exercise of extraordinary gifts does not ensure salvation, for many will say in the great judgement day, 'Did we not prophesy and cast out devils in your name?' But our Lord will say, 'Depart from me. I never knew you!' Edwards urges that the ordinary working of love and grace in the heart by the Holy Spirit is a far greater privilege than any of the miraculous gifts.

Edwards does not provide a systematic basis for the cessation of the extraordinary gifts as we find in Sinclair Ferguson's book on the Holy Spirit,[8] but it is convincing nevertheless.

With the rise of the Pentecostal movement over the last hundred years this is a highly relevant issue. Looking back, we can say that miracles have not been written indelibly on the pages of history like they are in the biblical accounts. Rather, claims made have been repudiated by the media and have often been surrounded with scandal relating to money-making and fraudulence.

It is a fact that there is a constant tendency to be preoccupied with phenomena. A weak faith desires proofs of God. A strong faith rests in the authority of Scripture. In revival there is an ever-present danger of concentrating on the outward and the external, to be excited about crowds or sensational features such as the conversion of a famous person, or physical healings. At the end of the day it is progress in sanctification which is of enduring value.

The most important issue for us to note is that revivals are not dependent on a restoration of extraordinary gifts, which is the position of the charismatic restorationist movement.

Edwards an example to pastors

I began with the assertion that every pastor is required to be a reliable theologian. His studies in theology will be foundational to his entire ministry. Edwards is an example of this principle.

All believers are theologians in the sense that they know God and study the Scriptures daily to know him more. The pastor is a theologian in that sense but is required to go further and be skilled so that he can rightly divide and expound the Scriptures. Edwards was indeed such a theologian. In addition he was a theologian like Ezekiel inasmuch as he was always on the walls of Zion surveying the scene in order to defend the city of God against false doctrine.

Early in his life Jonathan built into his devotional life disciplines of prayer, study and meditation. He was always at work. Most days he would attempt to be thirteen hours in his study. That is far above the average. In the end he paid heavily for this expenditure of time because he neglected pastoral visitation. That was a major factor in his dismissal from Northampton in 1750.

A constant requirement for the pastor is to arrange his timetable so that he can be balanced in the use of his time. If he neglects concentrated study, that will weaken his entire ministry. If he neglects to spend time with his flock, that will be a deficiency. He must take great care not to neglect his own family. Prayer is a priority and we will take account of that when we learn from the example of Martin Holdt.

Edwards made a pastoral mistake when in a sermon he decided to name and shame some young people guilty of obscene behaviour. This action alienated the families concerned. It is fundamental that the way to deal with bad behaviour is to go direct to those involved and hammer out the issues seeking to correct the offenders. We do not read of Edwards taking counsel from elders or church officers. The Congregational churches discarded eldership as unworkable. They regarded lay elders as simply 'not being up to it'. Nevertheless at Northampton there was a committee of eighteen 'leaders' which organized the congregational form of government by the congregation. With regard to eldership it is true that it is better not to have elders than have inappropriate elders. Those who have known bad situations can easily become cynical about eldership. However, the Scriptures are clear about the subject. We could say that many marriages do not work. On that account we do not discard marriage.

Edwards could have survived the offence he caused by inadequate pastoring. He could also have survived the fact that he did little pastoral visiting. However he could not survive the opposition he stirred up when he emphasized the need to reform the communion rule. Solomon Stoddard had taught that unbelievers could take the communion as a means of grace. Edwards was steadfast in the biblical position that the Lord's Table was for believers only. The members at Northampton were not ready for change. Edwards forced the issue by announcing that he would give public lectures on the subject of the Lord's Supper. The Northampton people boycotted the lectures, but some attended from other villages.

Resentment built up and moves were made to dismiss Edwards. A generation later Edwards was vindicated when the Congregational churches in New England reformed communion rules.

In retrospect the Church of Christ has benefited enormously through the theological disciplines and skills of Jonathan Edwards.

Every pastor should determine that he will maintain theological integrity and skill by rigorous study and personal devotion. When Edwards travelled by horseback to other towns he would write notes as he meditated on different theological themes and then pin those notes to his coat. He sometimes arrived home full of notes which he would then detach for further work in his study. May we be theologians who are constantly at work and constantly studying for the benefit of the people to whom we minister.

RECOMMENDED BOOKS

Jonathan Edwards, Iain Murray, Banner of Truth, 503pp hardback, 1987.
Jonathan Edwards, George Marsden, Yale University Press, 605pp paperback, 2003.
    Marsden's is a fine work. The story is told brilliantly. Murray's work is more astute on key theological issues. His biography is on a par with Marsden's. They are complementary.
A God Entranced Vision of All Things — The Legacy of Jonathan Edwards. General editors, John Piper and Justin Taylor. Crossway, 284pp, paperback, 2004.

8

Dr D. Martyn Lloyd-Jones

The pastor as preacher

Dr D. Martyn Lloyd-Jones was omni-gifted. He was a born leader and a brilliant chairman of meetings, whether in church meetings or in conferences. But he was preeminently a preacher. It was his care and his love for souls that made him an effective preacher. When he was leader of the large congregation at Westminster Chapel, London, it was not possible for him to engage in systematic pastoral visitation of the flock. However it was his custom after every service to spend about two hours in his vestry counselling those who needed his help. A deacon was always in charge to supervise this part of the doctor's ministry. Mr Micklewright was a principal helper in this work. He had pastoral experience himself and was ideal for assisting the doctor. Dr ML-J was a pastor by telephone to many other pastors. Much of his time was spent in advising and shepherding fellow-pastors, especially younger men.

It was his preaching ministry that formed the basis of all Dr ML-J's work. It was through his preaching that the church known as Bethlehem Church in Sandfields, Aberavon, in Wales, experienced

Dr David Martyn Lloyd-Jones

With acknowledgement to the Evangelical Library

a revival and was built up. He was pastor there from 1927 to 1938 when he began his ministry at Westminster Chapel at Buckingham Gate in London. He ministered alongside Dr Campbell Morgan during the 1939–1945 World War. The war severely depleted the congregation as people left London to escape the bombing. Campbell Morgan retired and Dr ML-J became the sole pastor. His expository preaching attracted an increasing number and gradually the congregation was restored to its original size. He preached at student conferences for IVF and IFES. I heard him give papers on many occasions and I was present when he spoke for over two hours at the Evangelical Library in 1962. The subject was the tercentenary of the Great Ejection of 1662. He spoke with passion. I never saw him read a paper; his method was to use an outline. Even when presenting a historical or biographical paper his method was to preach. His delivery was always personable and dynamic. He regularly preached at mid-week meetings and rallies throughout the United Kingdom. It was his preaching that was foundational to all his books. As with the English Puritans whom he admired and constantly commended, he preached his sermons first, and later, when they were transcribed for him from recordings, he edited them for the publishers.

Here I will first give an outline of his life and then concentrate on what we can learn from his example as a preacher.

A biographical sketch

Born in Cardiff, South Wales, Martyn Lloyd-Jones spent the greater part of his childhood in rural Cardiganshire before moving with his family to London in 1914. Concluding his education at St Marylebone Grammar School, he entered St Bartholomew's Hospital at sixteen to follow a career in medicine. He passed all his examinations with brilliance. In 1921 he was chosen as Chief Clinical Assistant to the famous Sir Thomas Horder, who was a cardiologist and the king's physician. The importance of precise thinking and analysis in diagnosis made a deep impression on the young ML-J. An acute intellect combined with astute observation of human nature and excellent memory were natural gifts which contributed much to his work as pastor and preacher. He could not put a date to his conversion. He came gradually to realize that he was dead in sin and found his only hope in Christ during the years 1923-24. By 1925 (and it is easy to follow his age as the twentieth century progressed since he was born in December 1899) he was experiencing an intense struggle over his calling to be a pastor.

In 1927 he turned his back on a successful and lucrative career in medicine and committed his life to the Christian ministry in South Wales in the district of Aberavon, in a church popularly known as Sandfields. Around this church was a population of about 5,000 living in sordid and overcrowded conditions. The church was part of what was known as The Forward Movement. The church was a refuge when sorrow or bereavement or trouble of any kind came to the people there. ML-J's salary was £225 a year plus the provision of a manse. This was in striking contrast with the advantages of a medical consultant who at that time could earn anything between £2000 and £5000 per annum. Part of his contract was to have thirteen Sundays per annum free. This was a feature throughout his ministerial life, namely the freedom to preach in many other places and also take time to refuel and rest from the relentless demands made on the life of a pastor. Initially ML-J was regarded as a lay-pastor because he had not been to a seminary and had not been through any theological training.

In 1927 Martyn married Bethan, who was also a medical doctor. She was under Martyn's ministry for two years before she really understood the meaning of the gospel.[1]

A remarkable work of the Holy Spirit took place in the church at Aberavon. The church membership increased in 1930 by eighty-eight, of whom seventy were converts from the world. The following year, 1931, saw another 135 added, 128 of whom were 'from the world'. All his life ML-J was a profound believer in the phenomenon we call revival. He always pointed out that the kingdom of Christ does not advance by business methods and worldly schemes. He never ceased to warn against shallow evangelism of the decisionist kind which lacks conviction of sin and heart repentance.

Upon his settlement in the Sandfields church he had to learn from scratch all that is involved in leading an assembly of believers. Very soon his calling as a preacher was recognized. In the first year of his ministry he agreed to preach in fifty-two other churches, usually on a Tuesday or Thursday evening. The impact of his itinerant ministry was felt throughout Wales. His preaching was powerfully evangelical. He was resolute in exposing the unbiblical character and destructive nature of modernistic theology.

In 1932 and 1937 'the Doctor' (everyone seemed to refer to him in that way) ministered in North America. His powers as a preacher were soon appreciated. Leaders in Canada urged him to return with a view to being called to minister to a large church there. He declined.

The record of these early years reveals many instances of his pastoral care of individual needy people, and sometimes the dying. He was a personal pastor not only in visiting but also in correspondence. Many Christians who lacked pastoral leadership wrote to him for counselling. On one occasion when his correspondence had to be forwarded to him, there were ninety letters that had accumulated in one week.[2] Not only was ML-J a born preacher, he was a born leader. Soon there gathered round him a dozen pastors. Together they covenanted in specific practical ways to promote the evangelical cause in Wales.

In May 1938 the Doctor announced his resignation from the pastorate in Sandfields and in the same month accepted Dr Campbell Morgan's offer to share the pulpit at Westminster Chapel in Buckingham Gate, which is only a short distance from the House of Commons and Buckingham Palace. During the war years the Lloyd-Jones family lived in Haslemere, Surrey. In 1943 Dr Morgan retired, leaving the Doctor as sole pastor of the church.

1939 to 1945 saw the congregation scattered and reduced to about a quarter of the size it had been under the ministry of Campbell Morgan. There are circular galleries at Westminster Chapel. The first gallery can accommodate about 720 and the second about 200. The ground floor can seat about 1,100.

The congregation was ignorant of the Reformed faith and unaccustomed to series of expository sermons. Some were opposed outright to ML-J and preferred Campbell Morgan's alliterative easy-to-follow simple preaching outlines. The Doctor's style was one which challenged his hearers to think through biblical doctrine, grasp it and embrace it. This situation was encapsulated in the remark of an indignant male attendee who went one Sunday morning expecting to hear Campbell Morgan only to be disappointed. 'I went to hear Morgan,' he complained afterward, 'and heard that Calvinist instead!' Some of the deacons were tinged with liberal theology. Overall the majority were content while the ministry was shared, but were not happy when Campbell Morgan retired. They did not relish the prospect of ML-J preaching at every service.

Under these circumstances the Doctor exercised exceptional wisdom. On Friday evenings he organized a time of discussion when the congregation could freely discuss any subject. It should be noted that a pastor will very soon know what the members are thinking when there is opportunity for open discussion.

Dr D. Martyn Lloyd-Jones

Some of Lloyd-Jones' friends were doubtful whether the primitive simplicity of church life in Calvinistic Methodism could succeed in London. One of the observers at that time was a Dr Johnson. 'When I saw that he was without choir, musical entertainment and any external aids set to preach the Chapel full, I wondered if he could — with his away preaching in the week — sustain the load.' At one time the weekly open discussion concerned what could be done to fill the Chapel as it had been filled under Campbell Morgan. Many suggested that there should be additions to the service. A minority expressed the view that the primary reason they attended was for the preaching and they did not desire any extra items.

The primacy of preaching is illustrated by the form of service followed. A chapter in Iain Murray's biography has the title 'Sunday mornings in the 1950s'.[3] It captures magnificently the form and atmosphere of those times for those who never had the privilege of being there. There were no accessories. There was a substantial reading of Scripture, a prayer of between ten and fifteen minutes, and then a sermon of about forty minutes. On the Lord's Day evenings it was the same, except that the main thrust of the sermon was evangelistic and would last anything from forty to sixty minutes. There were always four hymns in the usual Nonconformist manner. I cannot recall an addition of any kind whatsoever. During Campbell Morgan's day there used to be a choir, but that disappeared.

These years, 1939 to 1968, were momentous years. In the heart of London the Doctor exercised a preaching ministry the influence of which spread round the world. In addition to tourists who made Sunday at Westminster part of their itinerary, university students from many countries preparing for all kinds of vocations regularly attended Westminster Chapel. Also many students from the London Bible College attended Westminster. For them the Doctor was a model preacher. My wife and I arrived in London in

1954 with the express purpose of studying extramurally at London Bible College. I had just graduated as an architect and worked in an architectural practice in London. We lived at the Foreign Missions Club. There we met Iain Murray and David Fountain who together insisted that we attend Westminster Chapel and benefit from the Doctor's ministry.[4] We were inspired and imbibed the teaching at Westminster from 1954 to 1958. Our London Bible College studies (under Dr Ernest Kevan) prevented us from attending the famous Westminster Chapel 'Romans lectures' on Friday nights. The Sunday series that made a major impact on us was on Ephesians, a series on chapter three of Genesis and a short series on Ezekiel chapter 36.

In addition to his itinerant preaching all over Britain during the week and during the summer break, the Doctor was also in demand in the Student Movement. For example, his book with the title *Authority* was first preached as a series of sermons at a conference for students.

Throughout his ministry from his early thirties to age eighty the Doctor preached to congregations very much larger than those of leading preachers in the UK today. Besides his own congregation at Westminster, 1,200 to 1,400 on Sundays, there were the large crowds at the mid-week rallies or special occasions. For instance, as early as 1932 he preached to 6,000 in Toronto and in 1935 to 7,000 at Llangeitho. The Lord not only gave him the gift of preaching, but gave him the congregations which would benefit from this preaching. He was, without doubt, the foremost preacher in the United Kingdom during the twentieth century.

In 1941 a quarterly meeting for ministers began. This was by private invitation. It developed into the 'Westminster Fellowship' which was confined to full-time pastors. Sometimes subjects were addressed by a visitor or member of the fraternal but mostly it consisted of open discussion led by the Doctor as chairman. In 1967 I began to attend. There must have been about 220 who were eligible, although the average attendance was about 120. Some travelled all the way from Wales to be present. For nine months of the year the Fellowship took place on the first Monday of the month. Monday is the 'tired day' for pastors, but attendees would return from the fellowship greatly encouraged. To a number of members of the Fellowship the Doctor was a friend and counsellor, a shepherd guiding and advising them in their difficulties and encouraging them through their family and personal trials.

In 1968 ML-J fell seriously ill and resigned as pastor from Westminster Chapel. This brought to a conclusion thirty years' ministry there. He wrote to his friend Philip Hughes that he felt he needed to place into written form the material that he had preached, particularly on the book of Romans. Letters from friends confirmed this desire. A missionary in Mombasa wrote to say that he had read the monthly sermon printed in the *Westminster Record* since 1948 and another missionary in Morocco wrote to assure the Doctor that his written ministry had been a very great blessing over a period of ten years. For six months during 1968 the Doctor did not preach at all. His recovery from surgery was successful and in 1969 he was able to resume his very considerable and widespread itinerant ministry.

A significant event in the Doctor's ministry took place in 1977 when he gave the inaugural address for the founding of the London Theological Seminary. This was a seminary that had been established through his encouragement.

In 1979 the former cancer from which he had suffered returned. He was constrained to limit his public engagements, yet still kept a few preaching engagements during 1980 in Scotland, Wales and England. The Doctor believed passionately in the Puritan view that it is a Christian duty to prepare well for death. In his final illness he maintained an outstanding testimony and was an inspiration to his own family and the wider church. He entered glory on 1 March 1981, St David's Day.

Learning from Dr Martyn Lloyd-Jones as a preacher

There is much inspiration we can gain from the life and example of Dr Martyn Lloyd-Jones. He was the foremost non-conformist evangelical preacher and leader of British Evangelicalism during the twentieth century.

As observed, besides preaching three times a week at Westminster Chapel in London, he preached all over the British Isles and beyond during the week. This was to large congregations drawn from all denominations. In this broader ministry he reminds us of the prophet Samuel of whom it is written: 'From year to year he went on a circuit from Bethel to Gilgal to Mizpah, judging Israel in all those places. But he always went back to Ramah, where his home was' (1 Sam. 7:16-17). As a Welshman we can readily understand that he loved to minister in Wales. His influence there was especially profound. 'ML-J's sense of calling to Wales remained a constant throughout his life.'[5]

Five issues stand out which are of paramount relevance today:

1. The primacy of preaching;
2. Evangelistic preaching;
3. Unction in preaching;
4. Revival and preaching;
5. Systematic preaching.

Dr D. Martyn Lloyd-Jones

The primacy of preaching

During 1969 ML-J was invited to speak at Westminster Seminary in America. He chose as his theme 'Preaching and Preachers'. Sixteen lectures were published by Hodder & Stoughton in a book with that title.[6] In the first chapter, 'The primacy of preaching', he analyses the reasons why preaching has fallen from the prime place it should always occupy in the Church of God.

From the outset we have to keep in mind what preaching really is. It is addressing people in the name of the Triune God through the Bible and addressing them in the whole of their being: intellect, affections, conscience and will. Gospel preaching is the earnest endeavour to persuade people and move them to repentance from sin and faith in the Lord Jesus Christ. Gospel preaching is unique inasmuch as it can only be effective by the power of the Holy Spirit. Hence the place of prayer and holiness in the life of the preacher is paramount.

The Doctor always commended the English Puritans and, like them, he believed in preaching as God's way to convert sinners and to feed and sustain believers. Like the English Puritans he held that there is no substitute. Nothing else addresses the whole person, mind, affections, conscience and will, like preaching. Nothing else comes with authority from God himself. Nothing else is inhabited by God the Holy Spirit in the unique way that preaching is. The Son of Man himself came to preach, as did the one who prepared the way for him. The multitude did not go out into the wilderness to hear a lecture from John the Baptist. A rock formed his pulpit and the heavens his sounding board. He preached. And when his hearers arrived John did not flatter them or set out to make them feel good. His aim was to bring them to repentance.

What makes preaching unique? What makes preaching different from political speeches? What makes preaching different from lectures in school or university? The answer is that preaching is addressed to the whole man: mind, affections and will, to convert him to God and when converted to move him to love and serve the Triune God with all his being. In politics the speech maker will try to get his hearers to vote for his party. In preaching the object is to constrain people to believe in and live for Christ.

It is a mistake to confuse preaching with lecturing. Lectures can be assisted by power points and overhead projectors both to impart information and keep attention, but that can never substitute for preaching. The use of an overhead projector tends to break the direct link between the preacher and his hearers. Overhead projectors are useful for lectures. Lectures can be informative and even inspiring. But lecturing is not preaching.

Preaching is God's appointed way by which sinners are humbled. No human agency on earth can bring about conviction of sin toward God. That is the unique work of the Holy Spirit as Jesus promised, 'When he comes, he will convict the world of guilt in regard to sin and righteousness and judgement' (John 16:8). Of course the Holy Spirit uses a variety of means such as reading and personal friendship and discussion or listening to radio or audio cassettes, but it is expressly declared in Scripture: 'God was pleased through the foolishness of what was preached to save those who believe' (1 Cor. 1:21). Note that in the eyes of the world preaching is foolish. Satan hates it because he knows that it is God's chief way of humbling sinners and saving them.

ML-J warned against the trend to allow entertainment to dislodge the primacy of preaching with musical items, songs, solos or testimonies. He referred to the new kind of official in the church, the 'song leader', who is supposed to produce the atmosphere. 'He often takes so much time in producing the atmosphere that there is not time for preaching in the atmosphere!' Preaching as the vehicle in which God's power is revealed ebbs away when distractions have left minimum time to attend to it.

> We are told that today people cannot think and follow reasoned statements, that they are so accustomed to the kind of outlook and mentality produced by newspapers, television and films, that they are incapable of following a reasoned, argued statement. We must therefore give them films and filmstrips, and get film stars to speak to them, and pop-singers to sing to them and give them 'brief addresses' and testimonies, with just a word of the gospel thrown in. 'Create your atmosphere' is the great thing, and then just get a very brief word of the gospel in at the end.[7]

Various influences are antagonistic to the primacy of preaching today. In the days of the apostles the Jews demanded miraculous signs (1 Cor. 1:22). Today many of charismatic persuasion think that the power of God is vested in signs, wonders and miracles. Even though nothing happens except in their imagination, this idea persists. But those who persevere in their calling to preach are rewarded in the testimony of changed lives.

The primacy of preaching is often usurped by 'methods'. Energies are exhausted in administration or in counselling. Effective expository preaching requires enormous discipline of mind and heart. There are several mega congregations in the USA where expository preaching is practised. Don Carson of Trinity College, Deerfield, maintains that he does not know of one effective expository Bible preacher in the USA who has not taken measures rigorously to protect the primacy of prayer and study (Acts 6:2). There is a balance to be kept. Pastoring and caring for people is vital but the imperative exercise of study must not be neglected. The Scriptures liken the expositor to an ox treading out the grain. It is taxing work (1 Tim. 5:18).

Ben Bailie, a pastor in America, is also a research student completing a doctoral dissertation on the preaching of Martyn Lloyd-Jones. He has contributed a brilliant chapter in the book *Engaging with Martyn Lloyd-Jones*.[8] He contends that from the very beginning of his ministry ML-J was hostile to mere intellectualism and opposed to the Victorian obsession to entertain. If he were alive today ML-J would oppose a new danger which is the development of family services in which a simple talk for children replaces the sermon. There are ways of reaching families and children without sacrificing our main gift of preaching. An analogy would be sending Nelson to the Battle of Trafalgar but locking up his artillery canons and allowing only hand pistols. Another is Paul telling Felix that he will forego preaching on righteousness, self-control and judgement to come, and instead talk about little children and bunny rabbits. For over 2000 years the Church has been enabled to grow children into adults without at the same time reducing the adults into children.

A Holy-Spirit-filled preacher will hold the attention of all age groups.

Evangelistic preaching

Mrs Lloyd-Jones used to say, 'No one will understand my husband unless they recognize that he was first an evangelist and a man of prayer.'

Paul Cook observed that ML-J had three styles of preaching. 'They could be described as his Sunday morning style, his Sunday evening style and his Friday evening style. On Lord's Day mornings he preached in an expository manner with considerable application and exhortation to believers having to live the Christian life in a hostile world. His preaching was in a low key with not much physical energy being expended. His books on the Sermon on the

Mount and the Epistle to the Ephesians were the product of this Sunday morning ministry. His evening preaching was in great contrast to his morning style. He was preaching as an evangelist and flighting the arrow at any unbelievers present of whom there were many.'[9]

Dr Cary Kimbrell earned his PhD with a thesis entitled 'The evangelistic preaching of Dr ML-J'.[10] He writes: 'ML-J believed the message was revealed to the preacher. After quoting the apostle Paul, "I received from the Lord what I also passed on to you," he added, "That is what determines the message of the sermon as such; it is that which the preacher has received. The preacher is an ambassador, not one who voices his own thought, or opinions, or desires, but who speaks the message of his Sovereign. He is the bearer of a message he was commissioned to bring."'

Cary Kimbrell maintained that ML-J 'declared that the message must be divided into main sections. First, the message of salvation, the *kerygma* (Greek — usually translated proclamation), that is what determines evangelistic preaching. Second, the teaching aspect, the *didache*, that which builds up those who have already believed — the edification of the saints.'

'The Doctor believed the perfect summary of *kerygma* was 1 Thessalonians 1:9-10: "They themselves report what kind of reception you gave us. They tell how you turned to God from idols to serve the living and true God, and to wait for his Son from heaven, whom he raised from the dead — Jesus, who rescues us from the coming wrath."'

'Evangelistic preaching starts with God. It is a declaration concerning God's being, power and glory. This in turn leads to the preaching of the Law. The character of God leads to the Law of God. All this is designed to bring people to a conviction of sin and to lead them to repentance. This in turn should lead them to faith in the Lord Jesus Christ as the one and only Saviour. That, in the opinion of the Doctor, "is the mesage of salvation, that is what is called evangelistic preaching… this should take place at least once a week".'

How many practise this evangelistic ministry? According to Gary Benfold, pastor of Moordown Baptist Church, Bournemouth, very few pastors practise this way. Pastor Benfold has himself followed this method for over thirty years, as has Peter Masters of the Metropolitan Tabernacle in London.

Pastor Benfold described evangelistic preaching as that in which the text or truth being expounded and explained is applied to the hearts, minds and consciences of unconverted men and women. It is preaching where their questions and objections are anticipated and answered, and their fears dealt with, and it is preaching where they are encouraged to the Lord in repentance and faith. He outlines five benefits of a weekly evangelistic sermon: 1. It helps believers remember the gospel; 2. It helps believers understand the gospel; 3. The good news of the gospel thrills the hearts and helps keep them running the race; 4. It encourages the believers to bring their friends to particular meetings; 5. It helps prevent young people who grow up in the church making wrong assumptions about themselves. Knowing the truth is not regeneration.[11]

Unction in preaching

The concluding chapter of *Preaching and Preachers* is titled 'In demonstration of the Spirit and of power' and is devoted to the subject of unction. The Doctor felt passionately about this issue which is grossly neglected today. It used to be the custom in many churches before worship services for prayer to be offered in the vestry (elders and deacons) with this factor of the power of the Spirit in mind. This is how the Doctor begins the concluding chapter:

> *I have kept and reserved to this last lecture what is after all the greatest essential in connection with preaching, and that is the unction and the anointing of the Holy Spirit. It may seem odd to some that I keep the most important thing of all to the end instead of starting with it. My reason for doing so is that I believe that if we do, or attempt to do, all I have been saying first, then the unction will come upon it. I have already pointed out that some men fall into the error of relying upon the unction only, and neglect to do all they can by way of preparation. The right way to look upon the unction of the Spirit is to think of it as that which comes upon the preparation. There is an Old Testament incident which provides a ready illustration to show this relationship. It is the story of Elijah facing the false prophets of Israel on Mount Carmel. We are told that Elijah built an altar, and then he killed a bullock and cut it in pieces and put the pieces on the wood. Then, having done that, he prayed for the fire to descend; and the fire fell. That is the order.*

Jesus said, 'But you will receive power when the Holy Spirit comes on you' (Acts 1:8). That promise was fulfilled on the day of Pentecost when Peter who had been restored after his grievous fall preached with both clarity and power. The evidence of that power is seen in the 3000 who were converted that day. That power of the Holy Spirit is not confined to the day of Pentecost. Throughout the history of the Church there have been those who have preached with great unction and many conversions. For instance, to read the life of George Whitefield is to read of a preacher endued with the power of the Holy Spirit. Whitefield was all life, wing, power, force! Times of revival are times of the Spirit's power. It is

not always like that. The life of Dr ML-J is an example to us all
of one who preached in times when there were many conversions
and who persevered through lean times such as the early years at
Westminster Chapel. Perseverance is of the essence of the pastoral
and preaching ministry. Whether the preacher experiences little
unction or much, he must always do his best as the Scripture says,
'Do your best [spoudazo means be zealous, be busy, be industrious]
to present yourself to God as one approved, a workman who does
not need to be ashamed and who correctly handles the word of
truth' (2 Tim. 2:15).

The Doctor advocated the baptism of the Holy Spirit as a power
experience. Many differ with him as to the terminology and use
of the idea of a second experience after conversion but we would
surely agree with his emphasis on the need for spiritual power in
ministry and preaching. Whether we use the term 'baptism of the
Spirit' or 'filling of the Holy Spirit' the outcome of empowering
is the same. I conclude with the Doctor reasoning this out in his
book *Preaching and Preachers*.

> But look again at Acts 4:7. Here are Peter and John on trial
> before the Sanhedrin, and charges are brought against them:
> 'When they had set them in the midst, they asked, By what
> power, or by what name have ye done this?' But notice what
> the record has to say: 'Then Peter, filled with the Holy Ghost,
> said unto them, Ye rulers of the people.'
>
> How do you interpret that? Why does it say, 'Then Peter, filled
> with the Holy Spirit'? You might argue, 'But was he not filled
> with the Holy Ghost on the Day of Pentecost as the other men
> were?' Of course he was. What then was the point of repeating
> it here? There is only one adequate explanation of this. It is
> not just a reminder of the fact that he had been baptised with
> the Spirit on the Day of Pentecost. There is no purpose in the

use of this expression unless it means that he received a fresh accession of power. He was in a critical position. Here he was on trial with John, indeed the gospel and the entire Christian Church were on trial, and he needed some new, fresh power to witness positively and to refute the persecutors — some new, fresh power, and it is given him. So the expression is used, 'Peter, filled with the Holy Ghost'. This was another filling for this special task.

There is yet another example of this in that same fourth chapter of Acts in verse 31. There were all the members of the Church praying, in fear, at the threatening of the authorities who were trying to exterminate the Church. Then this is what happened, 'And when they had prayed, the place was shaken where they were assembled together; and they were all filled with the Holy Ghost' — the same people again. They all had been filled with the Holy Ghost on the Day of Pentecost, and Peter and John on subsequent occasions also; but here the entire company is filled again with the Holy Ghost. It is obvious, therefore, that this is something which can be repeated many times.

The Doctor in the chapter from which the above is cited goes on to describe a number of examples of empowerment especially from the Great Awakening of the eighteenth century to drive home his point that the Holy Spirit anoints or fills preachers with power. This occurs sometimes with remarkable results. From an earlier period, 1630, he cites the case of John Livingstone who preached at a special gathering at Kirk O'Shotts between Glasgow and Edinburgh. Five hundred people were added to the churches in that locality as an outcome of that one sermon! What shall we say in conclusion to the need for unction in preaching? The pastor is to seek that earnestly and to expect the Lord to empower his preaching. As Elijah laid the sacrifice on the altar and then prayed for fire to come down from heaven so the pastor should look for the fire to come down from heaven to bless and prosper his ministry in the saving of souls and the building up of the saints.

This subject is most relevant today. There are young ministers who are well trained and theologically reliable but if you challenge them about unction they look mystified and hardly know what you are talking about. To them if a sermon is biblical and well structured and delivered with clarity that is all that is required. The dimension of Holy Spirit empowerment is strange to them.

Revival and preaching

How does revival relate to preaching? There is a difference between a preacher who looks for and expects the Holy Spirit to come down from heaven every time he preaches (1 Thess. 1:4-5) and one who has no such expectation.

In commemoration of the 1859 revival ML-J preached a series of sermons on revival in 1959. However there was little response. Little interest was shown in that subject. He believed passionately in the reality of revival, that is, fresh and larger enduements of the Holy Spirit's grace and power. Few evangelicals have that passion and expectation today. The more time that passes the more revival seems to be viewed as something belonging to the dim and distant past and something unlikely to be given again.

Volume 4 of the Doctor's series of sermons on Ephesians 4:1-16 has the title 'Christian Unity'. Even though it is only marginally connected to the theme of unity ML-J breaks into the series with a complete sermon on revival. In this exposition he asserts:

There is no subject which is of greater importance, or of greater urgency, for the consideration of the Christian Church today than this subject of revival. If I have any understanding of the times, if I have any understanding of the biblical teaching concerning the nature of the Church, and the work of the Holy Spirit, I do not hesitate to assert that the only hope for the Church at the present time lies in Revival. I see no hope in any kind of movement or organisation or any special effort planned by men. The one supreme need of the Church is Revival.

He then goes on to define revival as a repetition in some degree or in some measure of that which happened on the Day of Pentecost. The spiritual awakenings of the twentieth century in countries such as Korea, China, Indonesia, Ethiopia, Sudan, Romania, Nepal and Sarawak show these convictions to be correct.

Although he never attempted to organize a Concert of Prayer for revival the Doctor was close to the theology of Jonathan Edwards on that subject. Edwards believed (see his book *The History of Redemption*) that this world will eventually be evangelized from one end to the other through outpourings of the Holy Spirit. The Doctor was not as optimistic as that but his view of the importance of revival in church history is beyond question.

This emphasis in ML-J's ministry is confirmed in an excellent chapter by Ian Randall in the book *Engaging with Martyn Lloyd-Jones*. The following three paragraphs are cited from that chapter.

In 1959, after noting that only six per cent of the population attended church regularly, Lloyd-Jones made this point strongly: 'What is needed is some mighty demonstration of the power of God, some enactment of the Almighty, that will compel people to pay attention, and to look, and to listen. And the history of all the revivals of the past indicates so clearly that that is invariably the effect of revival, without any exception at all.' He added dramatically, 'When God acts, he can do more in a minute than man with his organising can do in fifty years.'

In 1968 he stated: 'It is only since the decline of Calvinism that revivals have become less and less frequent. The more powerful Calvinism is the more likely you are to have a spiritual revival and re-awakening. It follows of necessity from the doctrine … you know that you are entirely dependent on God. That is why you pray to him and you plead with him and you argue, and you reason with him.'[12]

In his 1959 sermons on revival, he addressed the question: Why pray for revival? His first reason was: a concern for the glory of God.[13]

We must do everything possible to promote the gospel at home and abroad and at the same time pray with passion for revival. That in essence was the view of ML-J.

Foundational to the Doctor's life was the practice of taking time every day for daily Bible reading and prayer. Family prayer marked the close of every day. More than ever we need to give serious attention to our standards of devotional life and to the fruit of the Spirit.

Systematic preaching

Dr ML-J mostly employed the systematic expository method. He would occasionally preach a topical sermon but almost always followed the method used by the English Puritans in consecutive series of sermons.

This method has great advantages for the hearers and for the preacher himself.

Through consecutive preaching, which is demanding, hard work, the preacher will discover that the Scriptures are inexhaustible. The treasures of truth are limitless. But the mining has to be done and the preacher is always in need of books. The element of study is illustrated by the example of Jonathan Edwards.

The preacher will not have to lose time searching for something different every week. Spurgeon explained that it suited him to have a different passage or text every time he preached because three times a week he preached to a congregation of about 5,500 and every occasion was evangelistic. He also possessed gifts for this which were extraordinary. There may well have been an overall loss because at the time of Spurgeon's death there was a dearth of powerful theological preachers. It takes time to build up a theological mind in our hearers and by far the best way is to work through whole books. For instance by preaching through Romans systematically the doctrine of salvation by grace is established in a most powerful manner. Likewise, by a series on Ephesians, the doctrine of the Church can be powerfully established in the minds of the hearers. This method is cohesive and not fragmentary. It is the method followed by the English Puritans. From them we have received the finest body of expository material in the history of the Church.

Apart from a few short paragraphs in *Preaching and Preachers* (see pp. 66ff) I have not been able to find a detailed reasoned appeal by ML-J for preaching through books of Scripture. I do not remember this important subject being debated at the Westminster Fraternal but someone may be able to provide information on this. ML-J's example must serve as our inspiration in following this method. The clearest appeal for the systematic way of preaching that I have come across in my reading is found in the volume with the title *Rediscovering Expository Preaching* in which there is a chapter by John MacArthur Jr. He writes: 'One of the reasons I preach verse by verse is because I could never produce such inspiring, clever, creative, topical sermons week in and week out. Spurgeon had an immensely creative imagination. I just don't have that, nor do many of the preachers that I know.'

'The only effective way of seeing the significance of a passage is in its context. Going through an entire book sets the passage in its context on its widest, deepest, and richest level. One other thought: neither the Old Testament nor the New Testament was written as a collection of verses to be thrown into the air and allowed to fall back wherever they might. Rather, each book has a reasonable, logical, inspired flow of thought going from point A to Z, with all stops in between.' [14]

As David Jussely, associate Professor of Practical Theology at the Reformed Theological Seminary, Jackson, Mississippi, suggests of systematic preaching: 'It encourages both depth and comprehensiveness in the preacher. Each year the preacher will be exposed to the vast and manifold configurations of biblical literature. He will be forced to deal with texts and interpret subjects which might be normally avoided (like those leprosy texts). Such exercises challenge him and keep him fresh, enthusiastic and humble about preaching.'[15]

The consecutive method also has the advantage of discouraging repetition. It is so easy for a busy preacher to fall prey to just repeating in a different form work that he has done on previous occasions. Also there is a tendency to go back to his favourite subjects and in this way be unbalanced and neglect the whole counsel of the Bible. Repetition discourages the congregation who think, 'Here he goes yet again!'

During an African Pastors' Conference I asked the question, 'How many of you employ the systematic method of expounding books or sections of Scripture?' Out of forty only three were using this method. How to get started? Two articles addressing the subject of consecutive expository preaching appeared in *Reformation Today*. The first was in RT 89. That material describes the results of a questionnaire made at the Banner of Truth Ministers' Conference in Leicester. Many examples are cited with descriptions by pastors of their experiences in using this method. The second article appeared in RT 160 with the title 'The History of Expository Preaching'.

Martin Holdt

9

Martin Holdt

A contemporary pastor

A sketch of the life of Martin Holdt

Born in 1941, Martin was converted at the age of nineteen in August 1960. He was greatly influenced by the outstanding ministry of Victor Thomas who for some time was pastor of the Pretoria Central Baptist Church. Pastor Thomas was a student of the English Puritans and faithfully expounded Scripture. His godliness was evident to all. Martin testifies that Pastor Thomas was a role model for personal devotions and Martin set in place spiritual disciplines that he has followed and reinforced ever since. Victor Thomas advised Martin to cultivate the habit of praying aloud wherever possible. Martin says, 'This has been an enormous help over the years.'

In those times the young people gathered weekly for an open-air service and tract distribution. That is where Martin's preaching began. It was there that he sensed a divine anointing which ultimately caused him to apply for theological training at the Baptist Theological College in Johannesburg. After completing his course he was called to serve in a very small church in Pietersburg (now called Polokwane) which is a town situated about 160 miles north of Pretoria. There were only sixteen members, but this assembly grew in the two and a half years that Martin spent with them. He was then called to be the Baptist Union's first home missions minister, which is another way of saying church planter. By God's grace he was enabled to plant churches in Tzaneen, Phalaborwa and Newcastle, before being called to an established church in East London in the Cape Province. Following that, he was called by the Lynnwood Baptist Church to plant another church in the eastern suburbs at Constantia Park in Pretoria, a church from which he retired in 2011. Previously he had spent nine years building up a church near Johannesburg which had declined in numbers.

Constantia Park Baptist Church, Pretoria, exercises a wide ministry. There are several daughter churches which are being supported in one way or another. Martin has also experienced the joy of guiding and placing pastors in pastorless churches.

Martin embraced the doctrines of grace when he had been in the pastorate for little more than a year. He had been struggling with the doctrine of election. Martin was given excellent books to read in the early days when he lived in Pietersburg. His coming to the doctrines of grace was not an intellectual step only, but rather consisted of profound spiritual experience. One morning in his study he realized that just as the doctrine of the Trinity is beyond comprehension, so is the doctrine of election. When Martin embraced the doctrines of grace, peace flooded his heart. He went to the kitchen to announce to his wife that he now believed the doctrine of election. She was shocked! 'What about my Dad?' she asked. Her father was a hardened unbeliever. Unpremeditated, Martin responded with the following words, 'If it is up to your Dad, you know as well as I do that he will never be converted. But if it is up to God, there is hope.' She saw that. Gradually she too came to

love and to believe the
doctrines of grace.
Sovereign grace has
been an anchor and
source of strength in
Martin's ministry.

Asked to describe the
best experience of his
forty-four years of
pastoral experience
he recalled the time
when he had been ap-
pointed by the Baptist

Union to be a church planter. He settled in a copper mining town,
where he experienced fierce spiritual opposition. This was so intense that he nearly gave up. He was so anxious to see the church
established and prosper that he committed himself to two days of
prayer and fasting a week. The breakthrough came suddenly one
day in May 1970, and it lasted for at least another eighteen months.
Many were soundly converted and still stand today. Martin declared that he learned more about the fight of faith and the importance of sound doctrine in those two years than in any other
period of his life.

It was Martin's daily practice to retire early at 9.00pm and to rise
for prayer and Bible study at 3.00 every morning. This not only
gave him an extensive uninterrupted time for Bible reading,
prayer, preparation and study, but empowered him spiritually. Not
everyone can survive with this kind of regime but Martin was gifted
with a metabolism that enabled him to live with this timetable.

Martin always endeavoured to evangelize one on one to individuals
at every possible opportunity. He kept Bibles in his car, which

he gave out liberally to those who responded positively. It was necessary for him to carry a few Bibles in some of South Africa's eleven languages. A friend remembers an occasion when he drove a considerable distance to procure a Bible and then return to give it to a person in need. He encouraged all believers to spread the word of life of the gospel.

In his early years as a pastor he wanted to keep his weight under control and thought that running a few times around an area of two tennis courts would do the trick. Two serious marathon athletes on one of their training runs observed the strange sight of a man running round the inside circumference of two tennis courts. They stopped to ask him why he was doing this. When Martin explained they said, 'That will never work. Join us and we will take you on our cross country course which includes Thrombosis Hill!' Martin agreed. After a few outings the two athletes suggested to Martin that his running style was very economic and if he trained he would within a year beat them in marathons. This proved to be correct, and Martin took up marathon running seriously. Eventually he achieved the excellent time of two hours fifty minutes for the standard twenty-six-mile marathon.

Constantia Park Baptist Church (CPBC) was a church plant encouraged by the Lynnwood Reformed Baptist Church in 1981. CPBC began with only fifteen people who met in Martin's double garage. The numbers soon picked up and the assembly moved to a school hall. The Lynnwood Baptist Church then donated a site to the Constantia Church, although finance was needed for a building. This was a great challenge of faith. The architect, David Cowan, drew up plans for a building, and suggested that they should begin with a small hall to seat about fifty people. However, the group decided to take it a step further and in faith build an entire complex consisting of an auditorium to seat 250 people and a church hall, kitchen and other facilities.

At that point the church was committed to much prayer including fasting, and God's faithfulness made an indelible impression upon their souls. For example, a widow who was soon to have an investment mature could not sleep and in the early hours of the morning sought the face of God. She was persuaded to give the entire investment towards the building of the complex! Then the city council informed the church secretary that they were going to expropriate a large piece of the property intended for parking for the purpose of a future road. This would mean that the parking facilities would be severely curtailed. The church was paid out a very handsome sum of money for land for the road. Then the city council decided to shelve the road building project and the church was given the use of the entire piece of expropriated land at no cost! The building of the complex went ahead and subsequently the building has been enlarged.

After seven years Martin and his wife Beryl relocated to the Emmanuel Baptist Church, west of Johannesburg. For nine years they experienced much blessing, and the Emmanuel Church grew consistently. Two Sunday morning services were both packed to capacity as well as the evening service. Many were added to the church. However, Beryl suffered from cancer and was called home to be with the Lord in September 1996.

Martin then moved to Hermanus to pastor an interdenominational church where he was the pastor for two and a half years. There were a number of conversions during the time at Hermanus, including that of one of the team of specialists who performed the first heart transplant in Cape Town. Martin married Elsabé du Plessis, who is an anaesthetist.

The call came to return to Constantia Park which is a missionary-minded church. Every Lord's Day during one of the services there is a focus on a country from a missionary perspective. Constantia

Park has been responsible for church plants in Birchleigh, Kempton Park and in Elardus Park.

While on the subject of Constantia Park Baptist Church, Martin wrote as follows: 'It is important to share something which seems to be unique in the sense of calling a successor following my announcement of the termination of my ministry. It is my conviction that if a pastor has enjoyed a good ministry with the support of people in the church he of all people should take the lead in appointing his successor. First Baptist Church in Dallas had only three pastors in over a hundred years. From the outset the policy was that the outgoing pastor nominate his successor who would then be approved or for that matter disapproved of by the church members. The thinking is that nobody knows the church better than the pastor who has been with them and has faithfully served God amongst them and nobody knows available pastors better than he. Working closely with his elders he is able to guide them and the church to the appointment of a man of God who is approved and who is able and capable as a pastor.'

When he retired from Constantia Park Baptist Church, Martin filled a need in leading an Afrikaans-speaking church plant in Montana, a suburb on the northern side of Pretoria.

Martin always expressed concern for the Afrikaans-speaking people of South Africa. In recent years sixty per cent of his preaching ministry was in Afrikaans. This was on account of many invitations to preach in Afrikaans-speaking churches. Afrikaners are generally disillusioned. This group once held power and governed South Africa from 1948 to 1994. Afrikaners are criticized for the policy of apartheid. Present failures of the government are sometimes unfairly blamed on the apartheid regime. Afrikaners are often aggrieved and find no solace in the major Afrikaans church denominations which have been adversely affected by liberal theology. (For a brief history of the Afrikaners see the Appendix, 'Who are the Afrikaners?')

Under Martin Holdt's influence three ministries should be noted. The first is the Grace Conferences, the second is the Augustine Bookroom. Both have been the subject of exceptional blessing. The third is the radio ministry. He enjoyed much regular time with Radio Pulpit which has studios in Pretoria.

The Grace Conferences can be traced back to the year 1990 when a two-day gathering of Reformed Baptist pastors was organized at Mount Grace Country Hotel. It was meant to be a one-off mini-fraternal for the purpose of mutual encouragement. When John Blanchard indicated a few months later that he was willing to come to South Africa for ministry wherever he was needed Martin decided to ask him to address a similar gathering on the same subject he presented at the Carey Conference in England. The subject was 'Mobilizing the church for evangelism'. Blanchard agreed. In the event forty attended. A businessman who wanted to meet John Blanchard came to Mount Grace to ask him for permission to have *Ultimate Questions* translated into Afrikaans. When he found out the purpose of the gathering he offered to sponsor it to the tune of R5000 a month if it were repeated. That was taken up and the numbers grew to the point that there are now three conferences annually, two back-to-back at Magaliesburg and one in Cape Town. The conferees at these three gatherings add up to about 400. Many have been enlightened and transformed, and at least one Presbyterian minister has been delivered from liberal theology.

The Augustine Bookroom was a takeover from a book ministry which had failed. Elsabé Holdt took the leadership of this work. It was just at a time when the currency of the Rand went into alarming decline. Of inspiration at that time was the passage of Scripture where Elisha predicted a spectacular deliverance from the serious famine which was realized when a group of lepers came with the news that the Syrians had fled and left behind a huge booty. This was taken as God's promise to deliver the bookshop as well. The Augustine Bookroom did prosper in spite of the cost of importing the books. Today it is one of the largest Christian bookshops in South Africa. Visitors come from all over that part of the country to buy their books because they know they can rely on the quality of the materials. A hunger for and appreciation of reformed books is engendered by the Holy Spirit. Is there a reformed renewal in South Africa as there is in America?

Martin was rector of the Afrikaans Baptist Seminary. When he took over the responsibility of having oversight over the seminary there was an overdraft in excess of R30,000, and tudent numbers had dwindled to six men on the campus. There was only one way to face the challenge of keeping the seminary going. When Martin took over at the beginning of 2008 he asked the few students to join him in a day of prayer and fasting each Friday. Classes were suspended after a short tea break and time was spent in corporate prayer from 11.00am until approximately 3.00pm. The students loved this and at times even requested that the time should be extended. At that time God began to work. More students enrolled from the most unusual places, men of quality who show that they are called. Provision has been made financially to clear the overdraft and make improvements to the facilities. There is an emphasis on academic excellence alongside prayer, meditation, holy living and godliness.

The end of Martin's life came very suddenly and unexpectedly. In 2011 he preached at the morning service on Christmas Day, but after the evening service he felt unwell. On Monday he was taken to hospital for tests. He had just completed reading the book by Iain Murray on Archibald Brown and was excited about it. Tuesday came with the sad news of liver cancer. David Holdt, who is the pastor of Springs Baptist Church, said that when he used to jog with his dad in the mornings he was always urged to sprint the last 100 metres with him. David affirmed that is exactly how Martin ended his life spiritually. It was a sprint to the finish line. 'Who would have thought it? Christmas Eve we were all together with my dad weak but participating in the fellowship. The following Saturday he was in glory!'

Martin is survived by his wife Elsabé and five adult children, of whom two, David and Jonathan, are Baptist pastors.

Martin was a supporter of the annual Banner of Truth ministers' conference in Leicester, UK, where he was a visiting preacher, and at the Banner Youth Conference which precedes it. He was particularly supportive of churches in Germany. If he had been given two lives he would have spent one of them in Germany.

Recently Martin wrote an article in *Reformation Today* (RT 200) on the work of the pastor covering essential aspects of the work of the pastor. We will examine this but as we do so we should remember that the ministry is demanding and intense. The pastor must be ready to stand by the bereaved. He has to counsel and guide those who have marriage break-ups. These break-ups have disastrous effects on the children of broken families resulting in the need of great care and pastoral attention. The pastor has to shoulder the task of evangelism and the care of his people. Most pastors are expected to prepare three sermons a week. That involves constant prayer, reading, study and meditation. In addition he has to engage in pastoral visitation and this includes those who are seriously ill or in hospital. He has to prepare for weddings and has to preach at funerals. Every pastorate involves the work of administration and even though there may be godly elders and efficient deacons there will always be some administration in which he is involved. Guidance must be given, letters must be written and the inevitable e-mail be maintained. In addition to the above-mentioned factors there are unexpected calls. During 2004 Martin was called by the police to the terrible scene of a murder. A sixteen-year-old boy had murdered his mother who was a church member. Much spiritual help has been necessary to counsel that devastated family.

Martin expounds the elements and responsibilities of the pastor as follows.

The necessity of divine calling to the ministry

Martin begins with the call to the ministry.

I believe that it is absolutely essential to the success of the gospel ministry that those who are engaged in such a ministry know beyond any doubt that they have been called to serve Christ in this capacity, and that their calling is clearly recognized by congregations to which they preach. The apostle Paul states the case succinctly and clearly in Romans 10:15: 'And how shall they preach, except they be sent? As it is written, how beautiful are the feet of them that preach the gospel of peace, and bring glad tidings of good things!' (ESV). Charles Haddon Spurgeon, and more recently Ivor Powell, strongly recommended that anyone giving thought to the Christian ministry should actually flee from it until compelled by God to do what he calls them to do with no other option but to submit to his order.

The call to the ministry is first of all an inward sense of call. It is an irrepressible constraining desire to proclaim the unsearchable riches of Christ. Calling involves much heart-searching and self-examination. Calling must be tested in the congregation of the saints amongst whom the candidate needs to be well known for his godliness, his ability to teach and preach, and his integrity. There should be a measure of fruitfulness. We have to be cautious here as it has often been the case that excellent pastors have laboured hard and faithfully with very little fruit. Isaiah, Ezekiel and Jeremiah were called by God with extraordinary clarity and assurance and the reason must surely be that they had to persevere through terrible conflict and constant disappointment. It is said of James Haldane, a missionary to Morocco, that he was outstanding in every respect of his life and ministry but never saw one convert in forty years. The harvest came later. To serve joyfully in barren situations is in itself a mark of calling. Yet to return to the point, there should be fruitfulness in the ministry. If not, there should be an intense desire for the glory of God. There should be a desire for fruit, even agony of desire, for spiritual success in the ministry.

The necessity of reading and meditating in Holy Scripture

Martin maintains that he has never come across a fruitful ministry that is not soaked in the Bible. He writes as follows:

Some years ago, I listened to an American preacher who was visiting South Africa and who testified to the dramatic change and improvement in his ministry after a ministers' conference. When attending the conference he listened to one speaker after another making a variety of suggestions as to how to make the ministry more effective. He was unimpressed until an elderly man who was still engaged in youth work got up and had the audacity to chide the other speakers for having missed the mark! He asked them why they had not taken note of the significance of Joshua 1:8: 'This Book of the Law shall not depart from your mouth, but you shall meditate on it day and night, so that you may be careful to do according to all that is written in it. For then you will make your way prosperous, and then you will have good success.' He insisted that only solid Bible reading and meditation every day in the life of a pastor would render him fruitful in Christian service. The American pastor went home stirred and challenged. He began immediately to read forty chapters of Scripture a day! At the time of his speaking here in South Africa, he had scaled down to thirty chapters a day and was determined never to make it less than that. Yet within days of his beginning to read the Scriptures so extensively his congregation noticed a marked difference in his preaching. There was depth and authority. There was fervour plus wisdom and conviction. The church began to grow.

We must challenge ourselves about this matter. How many chapters of Scripture do you read daily? Have you set yourself a realistic quota which you are able to maintain? Of course it is not a matter of just speeding through chapters but rather one of digesting the Word. Perhaps this vital part of our lives is the very first exercise to be left to the end and thus to fall into neglect.

The necessity of a strong prayer life

Martin Holdt shares with us some practical details:

I have written into a small notebook all the things I wish to bring to the Lord when I spend time in private intercession. It consists of several pages, and these include the names of all the members and adherents of the church which I pastor, including their children. I pray for them each day because I sense that I need to do so if I'm to be a faithful pastor. Remember Samuel who declared, 'As for me, far be it from me that I should sin against the Lord by failing to pray for you' (1 Sam. 12:23). We sin if we do not pray for those whom God has put under our charge. It is unimaginable that anyone should be in the ministry who is not prepared to bring the names of all the people for whom he is responsible regularly to the throne of grace. This is absolutely essential.

The wisdom of rising early before the day's activities actually begin has helped me immensely over the years. Furthermore, when I pray, I pray aloud in my private devotion. Charles Haddon Spurgeon has helped me in this regard. The following quotation from his sermon on Mark 1:35 encourages this discipline:

'Certainly, our Lord Jesus Christ rose up early and went alone in the dark to pray, because he loved to put prayer first of all. He would go nowhere till he had prayed. He would attempt nothing till he had prayed. He would not cast out a devil, he would not preach a sermon, he would work no cure, however necessary, however profitable, until first of all he had drawn near to God. Take good heed to yourself my brother, that you follow the same rule.'

There is also place in the ministry for special times of prayer. Martin testifies:

The tremendous value of having at least one day a week in prayer and fasting has been a source of great help in the ministry. In fact, as I look back over nearly four decades of pastoring and preaching, the most fruitful times in my ministry were those years when I would spend two days a week in prayer and fasting, and experience the most wonderful mercies and favours of God in the salvation of lost sinners and in the building up of the people of God.

The necessity of study in the life of the pastor

We have covered this aspect of the ministry by making a study of the life and example of Jonathan Edwards but it will be a help here to note Martin's testimony:

I do not know what would have happened in my life had I not been given the encouragement to read, which older ministers urged me to do when I was young. It is and always will be a discipline. You have to make yourself sit down and read and you have to apply yourself rigorously to this task. It is most significant to think of the apostle Paul, conscious of his imminent martyrdom, wanting to spend his last few hours on earth reading, for that is what prompted his plea to Timothy in 2 Timothy 4:13: 'When you come, bring the cloak that I left with Carpus at Troas, also the books, and above all the parchments.'

One of the most helpful discoveries came through the ministry of John Piper. It concerns the fact of what can be achieved in reading in time-slots of twenty minutes every day. This was the suggestion:

'Suppose that you read slowly, say about 250 words a minute (as I do). This means that in twenty minutes you can read about five thousand words. An average book has about four hundred words to a page. So you could read about twelve-and-a-half pages in twenty minutes. Suppose you discipline yourself to read a certain author or topic twenty minutes a day, six days a week, for a year. That would be 312 times 12.5 pages for a total of 3,900 pages. Assume that an average book is 250 pages long. This means you could read fifteen books like that in one year.'

Or take a longer classic like John Calvin's Institutes (fifteen hundred pages in the Westminster edition). At twenty minutes a day, 250 words a minute and six days a week, you could finish it in twenty-five weeks. Then Augustine's The City of God and B. B. Warfield's Inspiration and Authority of the Bible could be finished before year's end.

This helpful discovery freed me from the paralysis of not starting great, mind-shaping, heart-enriching books because I lacked enough big blocks of time. It turns out that I don't need long periods of time in order to read three masterpieces in one year! I needed twenty minutes a day, six days a week.

Several other thoughts made the discovery even more exciting. Is it too hard to imagine disciplining yourself to set aside twenty minutes early in the morning, twenty minutes after lunch, and twenty minutes before you go to bed to read on various topics for your soul and mind? If not, then think what you could read! Thirty-six medium-sized books! John Stott says that an hour a day is an 'absolute minimum for time for study which even the busiest pastors should be able to manage'.

Many will achieve more. But I have noted that John Stott in his book *Between Two Worlds: the Art of Preaching in the Twentieth Century* suggests that the minimum reading would be at least one hour every day; every week one morning, afternoon or evening; every month a full day; every year a week. Set out like this, it sounds very little. Indeed, it is too little. Yet everybody who tries it is surprised to discover how much reading can be done within such a disciplined framework. It adds up to nearly six hundred hours in the course of a year.

The necessity of love

It is surprising that the importance of loving God's people is not brought to the attention of pastors more frequently. Love is a foremost attribute of our Triune God. He is love.

'A new commandment I give to you, that you love one another: just as I have loved you, you also are to love one another. By this all people will know that you are my disciples, if you have love for one another' (John 13:34-35). It is clear from the letters of the apostle Paul that he loved the churches to whom he wrote. 'For God is my witness, how I yearn for you all with the affection of Christ Jesus' (Phil. 1:8).

It is sad to think that it is a rare for a pastor to express from the pulpit his love for his people. If pastors do not give proof of the love of God in their hearts, how can they expect their church members to love one another?

The necessity of pastoral visiting

Martin declares:

> I have noted with alarm that in recent years younger ministers do not deem it an essential part of their ministry to visit people in their homes in order to share the Word of God with them, catechise them, talk with them and pray for them. It seems as if the thought is that the pastor's principal responsibility of preaching and teaching invalidates the need for visiting the people. The Lord's indictment against the shepherds of Israel clearly points to a situation where the people of God were not sought after and visited where they lived. Ezekiel 34:4: 'The weak you have not strengthened, the sick you have not healed,

*the injured you have not bound up, the strayed you have not
brought back, the lost you have not sought, and with force and
harshness you have ruled them.' In an average congregation all
the people, members and adherents may easily be visited over
a space of time, and every pastor needs to pursue this objective
energetically, heartily and lovingly.*

The necessity of daily watchfulness

The apostle Paul exhorts as follows: 'Watch your life and doctrine
closely. Persevere in them, because if you do, you will save both
yourselves and your hearers' (1 Tim. 4:16). This call to self-watch
is confirmed too in Paul's address to the elders of Ephesus: 'Keep
watch over yourselves and all the flock of which the Holy Spirit has
made you overseers' (Acts 20:28). Note the order in both instances.
Self-watch is primary.

I have noted that in this last generation there has been a higher
failure rate among pastors than ever before. Many, perhaps most
of these, have been moral lapses into adultery. Vast damage has
been done to the churches and to the cause of Christ through these
failures.

It was the practice of the English Puritans to keep a daily diary. One
of the main purposes of keeping a spiritual daily diary is to watch
oneself against spiritual declension. In keeping a diary it is good to
begin with thanksgiving. That is not easy when you have been in
the presence of disaster. But the habit of recording gratitude does
have the effect of reminding me that God is on the throne. Psalm
88 is a psalm of despair in which there is no thanksgiving. But
Psalm 88 is there to remind us that sometimes we travel through
the valley of death. Yet in our self-watch we must keep up our self-
watch as pastors. If we sink then how can we help others? A further

help for a pastor is to record in his diary biblical texts that have sustained and inspired him, and also verses of hymns. Some verses contain not only exhortation but compact truth. For instance:

> *O glorious hope! O happy state!*
> *Let not our hearts be desolate,*
> *But, strong in faith, in patience wait*
> *Until he come.*

Brothers in the ministry, Peter says that if we are faithful we will receive 'the crown of glory that will never fade away' (1 Peter 5:4).

Appendix

Who are the Afrikaners?

It is reckoned that there are three million Afrikaners out of a population of fifty million South Africans. In addition about 150,000 Afrikaners live in Namibia. Included in South Africa are the Afrikaans-speaking Coloured people (mixed blood) numbering about four million. They live mostly in the Cape.

Martin Holdt grew up in a home where German was spoken. In South Africa everyone was encouraged to be bi-lingual, and better still tri-lingual, and so be able to converse in one of the main African languages, Zulu, Xhosa or Sotho. Martin learned these indigenous languages and has always had the advantage of being able to speak to black people in their language.

Over the years the Afrikaans people have been noted for their skills as farmers. Many farmers settled in Zimbabwe and subsequently have lost their farms there due to Mugabe's policy of land-grabbing irrespective of the calamitous economic consequences which have plunged what was once the bread-basket of southern Africa into bankruptcy and unemployment. Many Afrikaans farmers have been noted for their Calvinism, for faithful Sabbath observance, and for consistent church attendance. As secularization has hit Western Europe so now many Afrikaners are falling away from their tradition of faithful church attendance.

To understand the culture of the Afrikaans people we need to go right back to the beginning to when the Dutch East India Company decided to establish a colony at the southern tip of Africa. The Company appointed Dr Johan van Riebeeck MD, a Calvinist physician, to be the leader. He was married to a French-speaking Huguenot lady, Marie de Quellerie. They took with them the *Heidelberg Catechism*, the *Belgian Confession*, the five-point 'Tulip' *Decrees of Dordt*, the *Dordt Dutch Bible* — as well as a commission from the Presbytery of Amsterdam to establish a congregation of the Reformed religion in Southern Africa.

Van Riebeeck sailed with three ships (*Dromedaris; Reijger;* and *Goede Hoop*). He landed on 6 April 1652 at the Cape which was the station for the trade route between the Netherlands and the East Indies. The primary purpose of this station was to provide fresh provisions for the fleets sailing between the Dutch Republic and Batavia, as deaths en route were very numerous.

When Johan van Riebeeck arrived he got down on his knees on the beach and prayed the following prayer: 'Oh merciful, gracious God and heavenly Father, as it has pleased thy Divine Majesty to call us here at the Cape of Good Hope to gather, with our own Council, in thy holy Name — may we make such decisions as maintain justice and, if it be possible, implant and expand thy true Reformed Christian religion in thy good time among these wild and brutal natives to the praise and honour of thy Name. This we pray and desire in the Name of thy dear Son, our Mediator and Saviour, Jesus Christ. Amen!' Six months later, on 14 October 1652 Governor van Riebeeck enacted measures against Sabbath desecration. Thus Sunday observance has always been the political policy and social pattern of South Africa.

From 1652 to 1835 settlers in South Africa came primarily from the Netherlands but there were also migrant and refugee Calvinist Protestants from Germany, France and Scotland. These, mixed with the Dutch settlers, became a distinct people bound together by the Afrikaans language. A significant number of the French progenitors of the Afrikaner people were Huguenots, the first of whom arrived in the Cape in 1688 following their expulsion from France by Louis XIV. It is easy to spot the Huguenot names by the prefixes: du Toit, le Roux, du Rand, de Villiers and du Plessis are examples. After the revocation of the Edict of Nantes, the flight from the persecution in France lasted for one hundred years. The faith of the settlers was Calvinistic, and their favourite confession of faith was the *Heidelberg Catechism*. A main feature of their religion was to stress on expository preaching, the Ten Commandments, education, a strong work ethic and the rule of law. Another feature was the remembrance of the ten days between the ascension of Christ and the Day of Pentecost. The Dutch Reformed Church exists in three main branches (NG, Herformde and Gereformeerde). The largest by far of these is the Nederduitse Gereformeerde Kerk.

After the Boer War (1899–1902) the Afrikaners found themselves in a depressed and poverty-stricken state having lost their farms and suffered terrible loss of life in the notorious prisoner of war camps. 26,400 women and children died in those camps through starvation and epidemics.

During the Boer War, captured Boer soldiers were exiled to prisoner of war camps in Ceylon, India, St Helena and Bermuda. It was there that they experienced very remarkable and powerful spiritual revivals. After the war the seminaries were filled with men who dedicated themselves to the ministry and to missionary work.

A mighty missionary movement spread across southern African countries. Gradually the Afrikaners recovered and in 1948 the National Party led by a theologian won a decisive victory. In order to preserve their culture and language they instituted the policy of apartheid. This, as we now know, was doomed to failure. In the political revolution of 1994 South Africans were spared a civil war. A democratic state was established. The African National Congress which political party began in 1912 took power in 1994 and has ruled ever since.

This reversal in which Afrikaner political power was lost led to discouragement. Many Afrikaners have emigrated to Australia, New Zealand, Canada and to the UK. In Pentonville Road, Kings Cross, London, an Afrikaans-speaking congregation meets.

The worst calamity, and one of greater significance than the abject failure of apartheid, has been the destruction of the once evangelical and theologically reformed Dutch Reformed denominations. This destruction has been caused by liberal theology which has also destroyed denominations in the UK such as the Methodists and the Baptist Union.

This terrible decline into liberal theology was first evidenced in the seminaries in the 1960s. It then spread inexorably to the pulpits of the land and has left many godly Afrikaners in limbo. Where can they go? There are only forty-five Afrikaans-speaking Baptist churches. By tradition the Afrikaners are not Baptist.

Out of the decline into liberalism of the great Nederduitse Gereformeerde Kerk (NGK) has emerged a new denomination known as 'Die Protestante Kerk' (APK) with 240 congregations and 44,000 members. There is poison in this chalice as deep-seated apartheid views remain in this body. One observer describes this as follows: 'I don't think that the APK has an official stand on race, although I could tell you that if a black or coloured person were to enter their church they would ask him to leave. While some faithful Calvinists may have gone to the APK, I do think the racial bias would have prevented many from doing so. I thank God that there are still some faithful men in the NGK. The sad thing for many pastors there is that they would like to leave but it comes at the ultimate price. Unless you have a 100% vote of all the people in your congregation, you'll lose your house, your income and your church buildings, for some even their cars. So many simply stay because they have very little option.'

It is shocking to think of turning people away because of their ethnicity. At an early stage the apostle Peter was just as intolerant. It was necessary that he experience the vision described in Acts 10:9-17. If the APK denomination studies the Word it is only a matter of time before the Holy Spirit enlightens them that the great commission is directed to all nations without exception. Pray that they will soon be delivered from prejudice which is condemned in Scripture.

Every nation is likely to have a small minority of extremists. This has been the case in Afrikanerdom. Politically there exists Die Weerstandbewiging (the resistance movement). This movement was formed in 1973 by Eugene Terre'Blanche who was murdered by two of his black farm workers over a wage dispute in 2010. Terre'Blanche was succeeded as leader by Steyn van Ronge. This movement is not taken seriously by the major parties, namely the ANC and the Democratic Party.

Notes

Introduction
1. William Perkins, *The Art of Prophesying*, Puritan paperback, Banner of Truth, p.94.
2. *Ibid.*, p.95.
3. *Ibid.*

Chapter 1
1. Essential is the requirement that the elder must be a 'one-woman man'. Over a lifetime in which I have been actively engaged in four ministers' fraternals in different parts of the UK I have noted that more have fallen into sexual sin than in any other area of life. I would say the casualty rate has been one in twelve. That is always catastrophic for the local church involved and for the family involved. It is the sin that stains. There is no way back. See John Armstrong, *The Stain that Stays*, Christian Focus, 194 pages, 2000. The statistic of one in twelve is similar in the USA. Also I have noted that the fellowship provided in a pastors' fraternal acts as a means of spiritual health and preservation. When pressures threaten to overwhelm a member of the fraternal these can be shared and be made a subject of prayer by the pastors. Pastors who isolate themselves make easy targets for Satan. We can take a lesson from lions. A pride of lions watch out for the weaker or younger animal in a herd of buffalo. By isolation from the herd the victim makes easy prey. Buffalo are notoriously aggressive and will attack lions. Films have been made showing how together they can rescue a stricken member of their herd. Returning to the realm of spiritual warfare it is never safe to be isolated. Pastors must ensure that they are not isolated from the brotherhood.

2. Kees van Kralingen. 'Full-time elders/pastors', *Reformation Today* No 229.
3. I Timothy 5:17 was debated in great detail at the Westminster Assembly. Subsequently it was the centre of a protracted discussion in Presbyterian circles. *Ruling elders — a sketch of the controversy* by Iain Murray is one of fourteen chapters in the volume *Order in the Offices*, edited by Mark R. Brown and published in 1993 by Classic Presbyterian Government Resources. In 1995 Poh Boon Sing of Malaysia published his book *The Keys of the Kingdom* (ISBN 983-99576-9-4). This 417-page study argues for Independency in lieu of Presbyterian or Episcopal Church government. Poh reasons cogently for full-time pastors as distinguished from ruling elders and uses 1 Timothy 5:17 as a key text supporting his view. With regard to this book I note that too soon Independency declines into isolation. Unity is the underlying strength of Presbyterianism. I have observed that Baptist pastors revert to Presbyterianism not because of infant baptism which rests on flimsy reasoning, but because of security. The best way forward for Reformed Baptists is to follow the *1689 Confession of Faith,* chapter 26, paragraph 15, and to build strong associations as did the first generation of Particular Baptists. See David Kingdon in *Our Baptist Heritage* published by Chapel Library.
4. In this section which highlights the importance and dimensions of theological and practical training I follow an article published in *Evangelicals Now*, April 2012, written by Robert Strivens who is the Principal of London Theological Seminary.
5. I derive all this material describing Calvin's missionary work in France from Dr Jonathan Bayes' article 'Calvin the Missionary' published recently in *Reformation Today,* issue 231.
6. *Order in the Offices*, p.251.
7. *Ibid.,* p.252.

Chapter 2

1. Each of the Servant Songs is followed by an elaboration, 42:1-4 by verses 5 to 9; 49:1-6 by verses 7 to 13; 50:4-9 by verses 10 and 11; and 52:13 – 53:12 by chapter 54.
2. The translators of the Septuagint translated the Hebrew using the word *thaumazō* which means 'I wonder at', or 'I am astonished', *thaumasontai* (they will marvel). Alec Motyer observes that neither sprinkle nor startle is free of difficulty. Barnes comments helpfully as follows: 'Many will be struck dumb with amazement at his appearance;

and, in like manner, many will be struck dumb with veneration or respect.'

3. *Josephus*, Books X – XV11, editor, G. P. Goold (Harvard, 1963), XV11, 195-207.

Chapter 3

1. J. Gresham Machen, *the Origin of Paul's Religion*, reprint of 1925 edition, Eerdmans.

2. Cited in Robert Reymond's *Paul — Missionary Theologian — a Survey of his missionary labours and theology,* Mentor, 2002.

3. Henry S. Nash, *The New Schaff Hertzog Encyclopaedia*, vol. 8, p.401.

4. Robert Reymond follows Paul in all his recorded journeys as Luke describes them in Acts. He then seeks to reconstruct what followed thereafter. It is a noble attempt but the fact is that we cannot be certain of how it all ended in Paul's martyrdom. Reymond argues for Paul's authorship of Hebrews but even some of those who endorse his book in the prelims take that opportunity to disagree with him. My view is that we must concentrate on the materials of the New Testament and give little weight to tradition.

5. John Flavel, *The Fountain of Life*, vol. 1, p.321.

6. Commended are six sermons on Galatians 2:21 by Robert Traill (1642-1716). Pp. 157-242 (85 pages) in *Works* (four volumes in two), Banner of Truth.

7. John Murray, *Commentary on Romans*, p.20, Eerdmans, 1968.

8. OPERATION WORLD, *The Definitive Prayer Guide to Every Nation,* Completely Revised – 7th Edition 2010, 978 pp, Biblica Publishing. Jason Mandryk. Hardcover edition: ISBN: 978-1-85078-861-4. Paperback edition: ISBN 978-1-85078-862-1.

9. These points are expounded in detail in the chapter, 'The Golden Chain', in my book *Who Saves, God or me?* Evangelical Press, 2008.

10. I came across this quote in a little booklet, *Hit by Friendly Fire* by Michael A. Milton and published by Evangelical Press, 2011. Milton found the quote in *The Columbia world of Christian Quotations*, Grand Rapids, MI Baker Books, 2000.

Chapter 4

1. It is interesting to note that Oxford and Cambridge were constituted universities soon after 1209. See appendix in *Who are the Puritans?* Erroll Hulse, EP.

2. Bainton p.65. According to Atkinson (p.101) many distinguished

Luther scholars such as Boehmer, Vogelsang, Scheel, Wendorf, Stracke, Hermelink, Bauer, etc. the list is long, have sought with great learning to pinpoint the moment of Luther's conversion. Others, however, criticize any such pin-pointing.

3. Robert Kolb, *ibid.,* p.20.
4. E. G. Schwiebert, pp. 384-437.
5. Friedenthal, p.249.
6. Bainton, p.168.
7. *Ibid.,* p.185ff.
8. Robert Kolb, *Martin Luther as Prophet, Teacher and Hero, Images of the Reformer* 1520-1620, Baker, 278pp, ppback, 1999, p.17.
9. *Ibid.,* pp. 47-49.
10. Donald L. McKim, p.261.
11. Schwiebert, p.297.
12. See article by Erroll Hulse in *Reformation Today,* number 172.
13. James Atkinson, p.132ff.
14. Fred W. Meuser on *Luther as Preacher of the Word of God,* in essays on Martin Luther edited by Donald K. McKim, Cambridge University Press, 2003, p.137.
15. *Ibid.,* p.146ff.
16. Nembech cited in Old, p.6.
17. Hughes Oliphant Old, *The Reading and Preaching of the Scriptures in the Worship of the Christian Church*, volume 4, *The Age of the Reformation*, Eerdmans, 2002, p.7ff.
18. Atkinson, p.182.
19. *Ibid.,* p.82.
20. Gunther Gassman on Luther in the worldwide church today in essays on Martin Luther edited by Donald K. McKim, p.289ff.

Chapter 6
1. Sharon James, *In Trouble and in Joy, Four women who lived for God*, EP, 2003, p.36.
2. Neonomian means that one takes personal faith to the basis of justification before God. While saving faith unites a soul to Christ it is Christ's righteousness imputed that justifies and not faith as a merit. Amyraldian is the doctrinal position which rejects limited atonement and is accounted as a four-point Calvinist position in lieu of five points.
3. For a discussion of Baxter's doctrinal divergence see Iain Murray in the 1991 Westminster Conference Papers. The title is *Richard Baxter*

Notes

— *The Reluctant Puritan.* This paper includes a quote from J. I. Packer as follows: 'As a devotional writer, no praise of Baxter can be too high; but as a theologian he was, though brilliant, something of a disaster.'

Chapter 7

1. Biography by George Marsden, p.369.
2. Biography by Iain Murray, p.450.
3. *Personal Narrative and Personal Writings*, ed. Claghorn, p.81.
4. *Praying Together for True Revival*, 202 pp paperback, Presbyterian and Reformed Publishing House. The book has a series of summaries and questions after each chapter which are very helpful.
5. John Gillies, *Accounts of Revival*, 1754 and revised and enlarged in 1845, Banner of Truth edition 1981.
6. *Seasons of Grace — Colonial New England's Revival Tradition in its British Context*, 352 pages, OUP, 1991, p.233. A valuable and rare book.
7. *A God Entranced Vision of All Things — The Legacy of Jonathan Edwards*. General editors, John Piper and Justin Taylor. Crossway, p.100.
8. Sinclair Ferguson's book with the title *The Holy Spirit* was published by IVP as a 284-page paperback in 1996.

Chapter 8

1. Iain H. Murray, *D. Martyn Lloyd-Jones — The First Forty Years, 1899-1939*, Banner of Truth, 1982, p.166.
2. *Ibid.*, pp. 244-246.
3. Murray, *D. Martyn Lloyd-Jones — The Fight of Faith, 1939-1981*, p.251.
4. Iain Murray invited me to become the manager of the Banner of Truth Trust in 1957. That publishing venture was born in that year. David Fountain became pastor of Spring Road Evangelical Church where he ministered to his retirement in about 1996. He was the first to invite me to preach. When I arrived he placed a Geneva gown over my shoulders. This was in imitation of the Doctor who wore a Geneva gown in the pulpit on Sundays. That was the only time I ever wore clerical garb.
5. David Ceri Jones in *Engaging with Martyn Lloyd-Jones,* edited by Andrew Atherstone and David Ceri Jones, IVP Apollos, 2011, 367 pages, p.60.
6. *Preaching and Preachers,* Hodder and Stoughton, 325 pages, 1971. These are the chapter headings of addresses given to the students of

the Westminster Seminary, Philadelphia. The Primacy of Preaching, no Substitute; The Sermon and the Preaching (in which he rejects the idea that there is much to gain in debating about God on TV); The Form of the Sermon; The Act of Preaching; The Preacher; The Congregation; The Character of the Message; The Preparation of the Preacher; The Preparation of the Sermon; The Shape of the Sermon; Illustrations, Eloquence, Humour; What to Avoid; Calling for Decisions (in which he explains why this practice is seriously flawed); The Pitfalls and the Romance; Demonstration of the Spirit and of Power.

7. *Ibid.*, p.123.
8. *Engaging with Martyn Lloyd-Jones* edited by Andrew Atherstone and David Ceri Jones, IVP Apollos, 2011, 367 pages.
9. Paul E. G. Cook in *Reformation Today,* issue 174.
10. The substance of this thesis was described in an article in *Reformation Today,* issue 136.
11. *Banner of Truth* magazine, issue 584, May 2012.
12. *Engaging with Lloyd-Jones,* p.97.
13. *Ibid.,* p.104.
14. *Rediscovering Expository Preaching — Balancing the science and art of biblical exposition* by John MacArthur Jr and the Master's Seminary Faculty, Word Publishing, 410 pages, 1992, p.340ff.
15. *Banner of Truth* magazine, April 2005, p.14.